Articles *of* Faith & Hope *for* Public Education

PAUL D. HOUSTON

Executive Director
American Association of School Administrators

American Association of School Administrators
1801 N. Moore St.
Arlington, VA 22209
(703) 875-0748
http://www.aasa.org

EXECUTIVE DIRECTOR: Paul D. Houston
DEPUTY EXECUTIVE DIRECTOR: E. Joseph Schneider
EDITOR: Ginger R. O'Neil, GRO Communications
COPY EDITOR: Liz Griffin
TYPIST: Sabrena Walston
DESIGNER: Jim McGinnis, Mac Designs

Printed in the United States of America.

AASA Stock Number: 21-00761
ISBN: 0-87652-231-2
Library of Congress Catalog Card Number: 97-75171

TABLE OF CONTENTS

INTRODUCTION v

SECTION I: EDUCATION OUTLOOK FROM *LEADERSHIP NEWS*
Japanese Visitors Witness Power of Diversity in Schools
    APRIL 1994 1
Survey Surprises Media, Provides Message, MAY 1994 5
SAT Scores: American Education's Success, JUNE 1994 9
Education's Problem: Not Bad Management, AUGUST 1994 13
Transformation: Key to School's Future, SEPTEMBER 1994 17
Many Reform Policies Based on Faulty Assumptions
    OCTOBER 1994 21
Santa Claus Mentality Means Lump of Coal for Kids
    NOVEMBER 1994 25
Money's Public School Praise No News to Educators
    JANUARY 1995 29
Block Grants Would Starve Nutrition Programs, MARCH 1995 33
Learning To Play Leapfrog in a New World, APRIL 1995 37
Use Data, Dialogue To Correct Perceptions, MAY 1995 41
Dear Congress: Can the Ties; Save the Children, JUNE 1995 45
If Not Education, How About a Children's Department
    JULY 1995 49
Racism: Deadly Disease for the American Dream, AUGUST 1995 53
A Car Wash To Offset a Waxing in Congress, SEPTEMBER 1995 57
Not the Whole Story, But a True Story Nonetheless, OCTOBER 1995 ...61
Information, Inspiration: Must-Reads for Leaders, NOVEMBER 1995 65
Rural Schools: Creating Education's Future, DECEMBER 1995 69
Ideological War Threatens Children, FEBRUARY 1996 73
More Needs, Fewer Federal Dollars for Schools, MARCH 1996 77
On School's 200th Anniversary, Threats Loom Large, APRIL 1996 81
We Must Reach Agreement on Behalf of Children, MAY 1996 85
Teamwork, Spirit, and the Absurd: 3 Summer Reads, JUNE 1996 89
How Does America Define Its Children?
    'At-Risk' Label Can Limit Their Promise, JULY 1996 93

Design Flaws in American System Make It Hard To Improve

    AUGUST 1996 97

Welcome to Another School Year—

    Another Election Season, SEPTEMBER 1996 101

Thinking Small Makes a Big Difference, OCTOBER 1996 107

Leadership Takes Courage and Conviction, NOVEMBER 1996 111

Election Points to Power, Peril

    of Education's Politics, DECEMBER 1996 115

Building Cathedrals—That's What It's All About, JANUARY 1997 119

To Spark Improvement, Make the Connections, MARCH 1997 123

More Than Good Coaching Needed

    To Cross 'Standards' Finish Line, APRIL 1997 127

Students Are Valuable Resources,

    Not Problems To Be Solved, MAY 1997 131

Summit Calls Superintendents to Front, Center, JUNE 1997 135

Celebrate Achievement, Not Scores, JULY 1997 139

School Leaders in High-Poverty Districts Have

    Three Strikes Against Them, AUGUST 1997 .143

SECTION II: ADDITIONAL THOUGHTS

Drive-By Critics and Silver Bullets

    Phi Delta Kappan, JUNE 1994 149

A Lens on Leadership

    The American School Board Journal, OCTOBER 1994 159

Making Watches or Making Music

    Phi Delta Kappan, OCTOBER 1994 169

School Reform Through a Wide-Angle Lens:

    The Consideration of Context, *Dædulus*, FALL 1995 177

The Blab Meets the Blob: Summitry, School Reform

    and the Role of Administrators, *Education Week*, APRIL 24, 1996 . .183

Administrator Accessibility: Invite the Wolf for Coffee

    School Planning and Management, JANUARY 1997 189

My father, who was a minister, used to tell me that his job was to comfort the afflicted and to afflict the comforted. I realized some time ago that that dual task is actually the role of any leader in any field. On the one hand, as educational leaders our task is to bring some discomfort to those who are too self-satisfied and to raise awareness that, no matter how well we may be doing, there is always room for improvement. All work is a pursuit of improvement. W. Edwards Deming and the other quality gurus are right, continuous improvement is the challenge, and the task brings with it a level of discomfort.

Many challenges are facing American education, from our outmoded organizational structure to our crumbling infrastructure, from the escalating demands of our economic system to the deteriorating conditions surrounding our children and our communities. We as education leaders can allow no room for complacency.

However, when we look at our nation's past and the tremendous progress our society has made — in large part because of the contributions of American public education — we have reason to feel good about ourselves. We should feel proud that we have advanced our country and carried out our historic mission so well. But, unfortunately, it has not been easy for us to feel good because so many critics have thrown stones our way.

Since March 1994 when I became AASA's executive director, I have been privileged to represent school system leaders on the national level. I have used the opportunity to voice the concerns and dreams school leaders have for our mission and the children we serve. In essence, I have been able to "fly cover" for the profession; I have been able to talk to the public through speeches and via the mass media. I have spent numerous hours on "talk radio" and appeared on local and national television. I have given hundreds of speeches to members of the profession and the public at large, and I have had the opportunity to write articles for different magazines and for AASA's publications.

I have been gratified and often surprised to find that what I have said has been read and taken seriously. Many of my columns have been reprinted in local papers and have been nationally syndicated. So, one day, when one of our members asked me when AASA would publish a collection of these works, I was a bit shocked at the request. He went on to explain that he uses the ideas in them and would like to have them in one place. My response was, "I never thought of that." I hadn't. But after having similar conversations with others, I became convinced that it could be useful to gather together in one publication the writings I have done on behalf of AASA to help our members comfort the afflicted and afflict the comforted. That is the origin of this book.

The articles in this book deal with many issues. But they are all focused on exploring one important truth: America's common schools are at a crossroads. They have served this country well and have served as a repository for the democratic ideals upon which this country was founded. And they provided a diverse workforce for an industrial economy. But as we move toward a new millennium, the economy is shifting to a service/information-based model. This means that in many ways the democracy will be harder to hold. We face the prospect of lacking enough high-wage jobs to offer hope to everyone. And we are moving toward solidifying a "have/have not" society where some can access their highest dreams while others' dreams dry up. Many people now have incredible opportunities, while others are faced with needing to acquire more advanced skills just to maintain their current job or to get one in the first place. Education must bring everyone to higher places of achievement.

Unfortunately, many people in the United States have lost faith in our governmental institutions in general and public schools in particular. As a result, the public schools, the part of government closest to the people, often serve as a scapegoat for a great deal of frustration and animosity. And folks are looking for leadership in a time when we don't particularly like leaders. All this has become part and parcel of an atmosphere in which school leaders are inundated with criticism, high expectations, intractable social problems, and shrinking resources.

We are, indeed, living in uncommon times. Yet, our mission must remain to preserve the common school, the one institution left that provides that mythical melting pot that creates a sense of common purpose out of a kaleidoscope of different races, religions, and ethnic backgrounds.

The preservation of the common school, as the key instrument for the preservation of our democracy, should drive all of us. Public educators need and deserve to be affirmed — and challenged. Our communities need our leadership and our engagement. Our children need our high expectations and our comforting. Our mission is to maintain faith and hope in and through public education.

આ

Articles *of* Faith & Hope *for* Public Education

Section I:

Education Outlook *from*

Leadership News

We hear a great deal about how superior other countries' educational systems are to our own. Yet few people ever ask citizens of other countries what they think about our education system. When I was superintendent in Riverside, California, I had occasion to host a group of visitors from Japan and see American education and our society through their eyes. The view was enlightening.

ॐ

Japanese Visitors Witness Power of Diversity in Schools

Sometimes in the hubbub and confusion of our everyday living, we lose track of what's important. Sometimes it's good to step back and take measure. A visit to my former school district by a delegation from Japan gave me that opportunity.

The critics of American education make much of America's supposed lack of standing internationally. Our students are compared unfavorably with children from other countries, and then the blame for our weakened economic condition is laid at the classroom door. We are told others do it better than we do and that we should learn lessons from abroad.

While I was superintendent there, Riverside Unified School District hosted 22 visiting educators from Akita, Japan. Since Japan is often held up as a country whose economic power is overtaking us, presumably because they are educating their workers better, I was particularly looking forward to their visit for what I could learn from them. And learn I did.

The first thing I learned was that they had chosen America to visit because they consider us a model of how children should be educated. In fact, their government had chosen them and paid for their trip over here for what they could bring back. The man who told me that kept a straight face while I chuckled.

How could that be? We know, because we are constantly reading it in newspapers and magazines, that the American public education system is a deteriorating system—a failed monopoly—that needs total rebuilding. Yet, here were 22 professional educators from Japan, sent to Riverside in America, to see how we produce such spontaneous and innovative children. I had to wonder why our critics have a hard time figuring out what folks halfway around the world seem to know: American schools are still the model for the rest of the world. It would appear that part of the human condition is wanting what you haven't got and thinking someone else has it.

In explaining the positive attributes of American schooling to my Japanese counterparts, I singled out two.

First, the American system is a system of second chances. We offer children the chance to fail without permanent penalty. Our alternative programs, adult and community colleges, etc., give children the opportunity to change their minds. Students who are not motivated early in their careers can change their approach and still become successful. America is the only country in the world that offers this open access, and little penalty for failure, to its people. This asset, ignored by so many, allowed me to escape early academic setbacks.

Second, the American system values diversity. At the same time, much of the challenge of bringing the many together has fallen to the public schools. This is where my lecture ran aground. The translator couldn't find a Japanese word for "diversity." This small detail highlighted the difficulty in comparing education in a homogeneous culture like Japan with education in the United States.

As our visitors went through our schools they had many telling and complimentary things to say. They noted how hard the teachers and children were working. They noted how clean the campuses were. They noted how friendly the children were to them and to each other. They noted how the children could continue with their work without being distracted by a gaggle of visitors with cameras and clipboards. They marveled at the children's independence: They wondered who organized the cooperative work groups and were astounded to learn that the children did that for themselves.

They raised two questions that I thought were particularly insightful into the differences in our cultures and how we tend to be better than we sometimes feel.

One of the teachers asked, "In which class do you teach the children to be creative?" Of course, the answer was in none of them and in all of them. Creative expression so permeates our schools that we don't carve a special class out for it. This amazed them.

The second question was even more telling. One of them asked me, "In which class do your children learn liberty."

"You mean history?" I corrected.

"No, liberty. The idea of liberty," he asked. I explained that we don't have to teach it, it just is. It is part of who we are as a people. I pointed out that our elementary school children will write up petitions to the principal to complain about the cafeteria food. He was stunned. At that moment I gained a new appreciation for what we sometimes consider a nuisance—the free expression of ideas and the questioning of authority. The expression on his face renewed my faith in this country and in the ideas that hold us together in all of our diversity. It also reminded me of our sacred duty as educators. Our task is to keep those ideas alive.

One of the final comments from our visitors was how beautiful our children were—and how different. It made me feel that if they saw the beauty in our children that we see every day, particularly the beauty in their differentness, perhaps our visitors went home with a pretty good working definition of diversity.

Sometimes, the best view of ourselves is through a distant mirror.

Talking about American education as if it is a monolith is dangerous business. So too is talking about it without data. For that reason, AASA periodically conducts studies and polls to find out more about what people think about education.

In early 1994, we polled the public on what they thought about schools, and also asked them where they got their information. What respondents thought wasn't surprising— those with the greatest contact with schools had the highest opinions of the schools. But where people without children in school got their information was highly revealing and makes clear that we as school leaders must find more effective ways of telling our story.

ે

Survey Surprises Media, Provides Message

R ecently, AASA made some big waves nationally by releasing a study by Mellman-Lazarus-Lake, done at our behest, on the attitudes of the American public toward their schools.

Much of the attention focused on the fact that the vast majority (89 percent) of people in this country gave the schools passing grades of C or better. Many of the comments and questions I have received from the press around the country have amounted to statements of disbelief like, "You mean people really like their schools?" It was astonishing to the press that most people give their schools higher ratings than the media and the critics.

Part of the surprise derives from the fact that people's attitudes toward schools are shaped by their source of information. The closer people are to their own schools—either by having children who go there, or by having neighbors whose children go there—the better they like them. The farther away from the schools they happen to be, and the more dependent they are on the mass media for their information, the more negative they become. This surprises no one who has worked in schools, but it seemed to astonish members of the media.

One of the things I found most interesting about the study was the fact that the American public has a greater grasp of the intricacies of schools than the critics seem to have. For example, the public was aware that the quality of schools is shaped by the social forces that surround them, outside the walls of the schools. Some of our loudest critics, many of whom have been highly placed in government, have not figured this out.

The study showed a longing for schools to be safe havens for children in a difficult world. One of the things I pointed out to the press is that over the past 30 or 40 years, we've moved from a world where "Leave It To Beaver" was reflective of childhood to a world where many children relate more to "Leave It to Beavis"—a problematic, if not frightening, challenge for educators.

Also revealing was that certain kinds of communities received the best ratings. Small-town and suburban schools were rated highest.

People are most concerned with the quality and condition of urban schools. Having been an urban superintendent for a number of years, I pointed out to the press that anything you want to say about an urban school is probably true. Urban schools reflect some of what's best about education in the country, but many are terribly impacted by factors such as racism and poverty.

It was interesting to note that those "other schools" (not in the respondent's neighborhood) continued to receive relatively low ratings from the public. But this opinion has actually improved by about 7 points since the last poll AASA conducted in late 1992. I believe a more positive message from the Clinton administration about our nation's schools is responsible for this improved public perception. Having a secretary of education who says that schools are better than people have credited them for, and that school problems will be solved with the support and leadership of school administrators, not in spite of them, does help enhance the public's sentiment about our schools.

The main message for school leaders, though, is the three topics of public concern outlined in the survey. Poll respondents believe we must address:

- **Violence.** This is no surprise to anyone who has been reading the paper or watching television. People are concerned about violence in our society and they are fearful for the children. I think administrators must address this in two ways. First, we must find ways to put this issue in perspective for our public. For example, last year nearly 4,000 children were killed with handguns in this country. Only a handful of these gruesome tragedies happened in schools. While schools may not be 100 percent safe for all children, they are probably safer than any other place that many children spend their time.

- **Parent involvement.** Respondents clearly believed that the lack of parent involvement was not because schools do not want parents involved. However, respondents suggested a number of ideas school leaders could use to increase parent involvement in their children's education. One popular idea was a homework hotline. This is a relatively inexpensive way of providing ongoing communication to homes using current technology.

- **Values.** There was a sense that legal and political issues of the last several decades have made schools back away from teaching and supporting core values. While respondents were not sympathetic to those on the far right who would eliminate discussion about issues such as sex, neither did they support an amoral teaching environment. What the public is telling us is that we need to make schools safe places morally, as well as physically, for our children, by reintroducing and re-emphasizing many of the core values that have been widely accepted in this country for the past 300 years.

AASA is committed to addressing the issues of youth violence, parent involvement and values in programs, publications and through other means in the coming months.

When we ask people for their ideas, they can surprise us with the depth of their understanding and usefulness of their suggestions. This is just the beginning of our campaign to share these ideas with you, and to continue to ask questions of our public, so that we can better meet the needs of America's children.

☙

Everyone knows American schools have declined; they know it because they read it in the paper. And what they read often is based upon test scores. The critics of American common schools have had particular fun pointing to the declining average score on the SAT as proof positive that American schools are in decline. But there is more to the story—much more.

❧

SAT Scores:
American Education's Success

I have often thought that the policy rhetoric around American education is a political black hole where the light of truth goes to die. One truth that has been sucked into this giant hole is the story of SAT results for American students.

We have been bombarded with an ongoing critique of America's schools for the past two decades as average SAT scores dropped from highs in the early 1970s of nearly 940 to the low point in 1982 of 893. This drop, often referred to as "precipitous," has armed a generation of critics who want the country to believe the schools are failing. Of course, basing any analysis on an average is a tricky proposition. It reminds me of the man who had his head in the refrigerator and his feet on the stove: On average, he was comfortable.

There are a number of problems with the analysis provided by public education critics. First, it ignores the fact that the "precipitous" drop is accounted for by only five items on the test. The millions of students taking the test are getting five fewer questions right today, on average, than did earlier generations.

More importantly, those testing wizards in Princeton, N.J., who developed the SAT have repeatedly made it clear that they were not trying to develop a measure of school effectiveness. The SAT was, and continues to be, but one means of determining potential college success. Therefore, for it to be used as a standard for measuring America's schools is a gross misuse of its original intent.

Critics of schools, such as former Secretary of Education Bill Bennett, love to point to the decline in average from 1972 to 1982, as he did in his recent report card on America's schools.

What Bennett and others fail to tell us is that, in fact, the average score went up during the 1980s from a low of 893 to a current average of slightly more than 900. At the same time, many more students were taking the test. In 1972, only about 31 percent of students took the test, while in 1992, 42 percent took the examination.

Because we must contend with this criticism, however, I decided it was appropriate to give you some tips on how you might improve the scores in your district, to get the critics off your back.

&. **Tip 1:** Don't let lower scoring kids take the test. Would you be surprised to learn that students who have good grades in high school do better on the test than those who have lower grades? If you have more C students taking the test proportionately, the average score will drop. We have spent the last few decades encouraging a broader spectrum of kids to apply for college. They then took the entrance exam. The increased number of lower achieving high school students taking the SAT has lowered the average score.

Researchers from the Sandia National Laboratory found that if you had only the same slice of the senior class taking the test today as took it in the mid-1970s, the average would be up nearly 40 points.

Of course, discouraging kids from pursuing their dreams is not very American and certainly not in the tradition of American public education. Unfortunately, that seems to be what the critics are implying that we should be doing. Rather than getting credit for broadening the children's dreams to pursue college, we are criticized because we have encouraged more kids to take the test.

Ꮡ **Tip 2:** Cut spending for education. If you lower your per-pupil average enough, your score should soar, according to folks like Bennett, who point out that certain states that do well on the SAT spend less money than states with lower scores on the SAT.

Bennett cites 10 states that do particularly well with less. These 10 average about $5,000 per pupil in expenditures while averaging 1,040 on the SAT. Proof positive that more money doesn't matter, and may actually be inversely related to performance.

There is a bit more to this story, of course. Bennett's favorite states average 9 percent of their students taking the SAT, while high-spending states average nearly 70 percent of their kids taking the test.

This invites a question: What do you want for your money, higher scores or lots of kids going to college? I might respectfully suggest to Bennett that he has his priorities misplaced.

Ꮡ **Tip 3:** Have your students born into wealthier families!

The highest correlation between high scores and other variables is family income. The higher your family income, the better you do on the test. For example, if parents earn less than $10,000 per year, the average is 767. If the income is between $30,000 and $40,000, the average is 855. If family income is over $70,000, the average score is 1,000.

Of course, all three of these tips are my humble attempt at satire. But they are no more bizarre than the criticism aimed at schools based upon bogus data and misinterpretation of fact.

The fact is, America's schools are grappling with a society that does not support its children adequately. Despite that, the results of the SAT, overall, are a positive story. More kids are aspiring to college and taking the test. The various ethnic subgroups taking the test are all scoring higher now than they did a decade ago.

The SAT story is one of the most positive about America's schools. Unfortunately, it has been turned into a nightmarish tale by our critics.

Let's stop worrying about the averages and make sure that all of our children have the same opportunities that those living in high-income families have. This would be the best outcome of all the focus on SAT scores.

૨૭

One of the most troubling things confronting school leaders over the last few years has been criticism from people who often don't know what they are talking about. Louis Gerstner, chairman of the board of IBM, published a book in 1994 that outlined how we should begin reinventing education. This from the same corporate leader who in 1996 spearheaded the national summit on education and barely invited educators to participate. I thought it would be useful to tell the other side of the story.

ॐ

Education's Problem: Not Bad Management

L ouis Gerstner, chairman of IBM and co-author of *Reinventing Education*, in a recent *New York Times* Op Ed piece entitled "Our Schools Are Failing—Do We Care?" once more demonstrated why it is dangerous for people to speak out on topics about which they have little knowledge or understanding.

Because of Gerstner's experience as CEO at RJR Nabisco, which included oversight of that company's foundation sponsorship of the Next Century Schools project, he has now positioned himself as an expert on America's schools, with a great many assumptions about how schools are failing and what ought to be done about them.

Given the state of IBM, his current company, one must wonder if Gerstner would not better serve by spending a little more time trying to figure out how to get big blue out of the red. The fact is, the problems with the American economy are tied much more closely to the management decisions that have been made over the last few decades than to the quality of American education.

To be fair to Gerstner, many of his prescriptions are very reasonable. He calls for better teacher preparation and the revamping of state licensing requirements. This makes sense and has been called for by educators for some time. He calls for classrooms to be transformed into problem-solving, hand-on exploration and cooperative learning settings. Again, this tracks with most education reformers' notions of how things ought to change.

He calls for a longer school day and school year for consistent progress. Again, this movement from the agrarian calendar to a more modern one is long overdue, but will prove costly. He also calls for schools that serve disadvantaged students to have more resources to take care of the job. This is also clearly a necessary and expensive step.

But while some of his solutions are on target, the assumptions he makes about why schools are the way they are are dead wrong and based on bad information. Wasteful management, falling test scores and graduation rates and a growing number of graduates who can't perform in the workplace are the problems, he asserts.

Let's examine his assumptions.

As a school superintendent for 17 years, I welcomed a number of community business people into the schools to tell us how to manage our schools better. They concluded that the schools do a remarkably good job of managing very limited resources. Approximately 6 to 7 percent of education spending is dedicated to administration. That is comparable to or less than what is spent in many other industries in the country. Educational management was "leaned" long before it became fashionable in the business community.

As to those falling test scores and graduation rates, the facts just don't support the assumption. Graduation rates have never been higher than they are right now. In 1950, back in the golden age of American business that Gerstner seems to long for, the dropout rate in this country was 50 percent. Today, the dropout rate is 25 percent. Another 10 to 15 percent complete school through alternative methods.

The only test score that has been falling is the "average" SAT score. The reason the average is dropping is that we have a much broader segment of students taking the test and going on to college than we had a generation ago. This broader pool of candidates has caused the average to drop, while the students at the top have consistently improved their scores. In fact, every subgroup taking the test has improved its scores, according to one study.

Gerstner also talks about the $30 billion in worker training lost each year to retool and make up for the poor literacy of workers.

While it is clear that the workplace of today is a more sophisticated environment requiring a higher level of skill than the workplace of a generation ago, it is also clear that the money business spends on worker training is not going toward literacy. Actually, about 85 percent of the money invested by business in training is going to the skilled and college-educated portion of the workforce. Only about 15 percent is actually being invested in the low-skilled "illiterate" workers of which business leaders often speak.

While Gerstner's foray into education is done with mixed results, he would be far more persuasive if he could get a handle on the real problem with American education—our failure to respond adequately to the deteriorating social conditions that surround our schools and the escalating demands placed upon them. Perhaps Gerstner and his business colleagues who are so critical of education could join hands with those who are struggling with these issues on a day-to-day basis. They need a helping hand, not a clenched fist.

વ્ક

In all the talk about *restructuring* and *reforming* schools, I think the real point has been missed. The fact is, schools need to be *transformed*. Folks want schools to be better, but not different. Yet, it is difficult to imagine that schools can truly become as good as they need to be without becoming something they are not.

Butterflies bear little resemblance to caterpillars. Schools of the future will, by necessity, look very different from the ones we have today. And much of this has to do with the issues confronting our children.

∂❦

Transformation:
Key to School's Future

This is the time of year when we lay out our plans for the coming year. Since arriving at AASA, I've begun carrying out what I think the agenda for a vital national organization of school leaders should be.

First, I've been criss-crossing the country, speaking out on your behalf to the media and to the public. My mission has been to debunk the myth that schools have deteriorated over time. If you've been reading these columns, you know that I have very strong convictions that, in fact, not only have we not deteriorated, we have been improving our performance for the past several decades.

That's the good news. The bad news is that we are not as good as we have to be, given the deteriorating conditions of our society and escalating demands of the workplace. These two factors call for us, as education leaders, to redouble our efforts to improve education, not because it's gotten worse, but because it needs to get so much better. This positive approach empowers people in schools to carry out the difficult work that lies before us.

But in addition to defending our historic role, we must move forward. It's time to develop a new mission for schools.

Historically, we have sorted children, providing for various levels of work in an industrial society. Because we no longer live in an industrial era, we must bring all students up to a high level of performance. More than just reforming or restructuring schools is called for. We must truly transform them into a different institution.

This calls for doing business in markedly different ways. I'm not even certain what all those ways are, but I believe we are positioned to lead this search.

A few years ago, I visited the George Washington Carver Museum in Tuskegee, Ala. Carver, as we all know, was a great scientist who created multiple uses for the peanut and almost single-handedly saved the agricultural industry in much of the South. What many of us do not know is that Carver was not just a scientist; he was also an artist. He would walk along the back roads of Alabama and gather up pieces of twine and yarn and stick them in his pocket. He would find unusual colors of clay and scoop it up and take it home with him. He would take the twine and yarn and weave them into beautiful tapestries and take that clay and paint gorgeous pictures with it. He was operating in a transformational mode. He was taking something of no value that was of base material and turning it into something of great beauty.

This is a wonderful metaphor for education. We are in the business of helping children, some of whom may have been taught that they have no value, to transform themselves to achieve their potential.

Many of you out there already are taking new and different approaches to education. We need to become a trading center for these ideas so that we can learn from each other.

As school and community leaders from around the country, we are positioned, also, to take the message of America's children and their needs to the people in powerful and persuasive ways. We must develop a national crusade on behalf of children.

We are living in a time and in a society that seems not to value its children. In fact, I often feel that we fear our children. I tell the press that over the last 30 years the condition of our children has gone from "Leave It to Beaver" to "Leave It to Beavis." This change in family structure and in the values that children are taught has played havoc with our social fabric. And far too often we blame children for the problems they have, instead of taking responsibility as adults to do something about those problems.

Part of our strategy to turn this around is exploring the concept of children's rights, such as the right to be healthy, to have a good education and to be loved and supported by caring adults.

We are also exploring the revival of a campaign for an investment trust fund for children. We already have a trust fund for the elderly, known as Social Security. Perhaps it's time that we, as a nation, gave the poorest and most at-risk segment of our population some of the same benefits. Right now, we spend more money on cat food than we do on textbooks. We live in the richest nation in the world, and yet our animals have a better chance of being inoculated than our children do. Therefore, investment on behalf of the children is called for.

Finally, I believe that we need to create a program of "shepherding" for our children. We as adults, whether we are in the media, parents, corporate leaders or members of the community at large, all have a responsibility for shepherding the next generation of children. I believe AASA can play a vital role in bringing this to the consciousness of America and reminding America of its conscience. Certainly it's ridiculous to talk about school reform without talking about reforming the conditions in which children live their lives.

School reform has taken many forms in recent years. First, we tried to do more of what we were already doing. Then we tried to change the power relationships. Now, we seem ready to begin talking about really making schools different. If we are to do that, we must be sure to make the changes that will really get us where we need to go. I have formulated five questions we should ask before we go too far with any effort to reform schools.

ॐ

Many Reform Policies Based on Faulty Assumptions

Ever since the early 1980s when "A Nation at Risk" told of a "rising tide of mediocrity in our schools," educators have been inundated with hundreds of reports on how we ought to be doing better.

While many of our critics would like to say that we've failed, or that we are deteriorating, we are doing better than ever. The problem is, we are not doing the job that we need to do because we are focusing on incremental improvements in an age of exponential change. The national reform agenda may fail, because it is based on faulty assumptions.

The so-called first wave of reform was trying to do more of what we were already doing. For example, if we had 180 days of school, some "expert" believed that 190 would be better. If six hours of school a day were not enough, then we ought to have seven. If students were supposed to have 18 credits for graduation, 20 would be better. Insanity has been described as a sickness where the afflicted does the same thing over and over again and expects a different result. If that is true, then much of our reform efforts in the first few years strike me as insanity.

The second wave of reform, or "restructuring," seems to be focused on shifting power from one place to another. Site-based decision making is a good example. Nothing is wrong with site-based decision making. It just doesn't guarantee that anything is going to be better at the sites than what's already going on. None of the research yet indicates an increase in student achievement.

The best example of the confusion over this is the position the unions have taken on site-based decision making. In some districts, the unions are embracing it and pushing it forward; in others, they are resisting and trying to undetermine it. A lot of this confusion has to do with perceptions about who's going to have power once the shift is made.

Vouchers for private schools is another attempt to shift power—the power over where kids go to school. Charter schools are another example of the power struggle.

Instead of talking about reform and restructuring, we really ought to be talking about "transforming" schools. We need to be making them fundamentally different than they have been historically. That means we have to create a sense of alchemy, where we're taking one thing and making it something entirely diffferent. But there are five questions we ought to be asking ourselves before we move forward.

❧ Will this reform do anything about changing education for the poor children in this country?

Our major problems revolve around our inability to do an adequate job of educating poor children. We do an excellent job educating students in the upper third, and they can compete with anyone in the world; the middle third of our population tend to do quite well and are very successful; but our bottom third is where we have serious problems. If reforms don't address this bottom third, then we should be questioning why we are pursuing them.

❧ Where is the burden of "reform" being placed?

So many of the reforms that we've pursued over the last decade have placed the burden on the children. No pass, no play is an example of this. If children don't meet the standard, then they can't participate in extracurricular activities. The burden of reform in a school setting should be placed on the adults, not on the children. Children should not be further penalized because adults aren't doing their jobs.

❧ Will the money be available to do the reform as it is being proposed?

We have a wonderful set of national goals in this country that we are pursuing for the year 2000. One of these goals is that all children should come to school ready to learn. This is a formidable goal, yet one that must be attained if we are to meet the others. But does anyone seriously believe that we're willing to spend the estimated $30 billion it will take to pursue this goal? Until we are willing to get serious about putting dollars behind these reforms, then we have to question how serious we are about the reforms themselves.

❧ Does the reform prepare children for the next century?

Many reforms are really aimed at educating kids for the 1950s. Our kids are facing a very different world than the one in which we grew up. If the reforms aren't addressing the issue of preparing children for a world of ambiguity and uncertainty, then we have to question, again, whether the reforms are worth the effort.

❧ Will the reform touch the inside of the classroom?

This seems an obvious question, but many national reform efforts never really touch the classroom. They are reforms of structure in the system or reforms in policies or procedures that don't change how teachers interact with children.

❧

My personal title for this column was "No, Virginia, there is no Santa Claus." I wrote it right after the 1994 elections. The "Contract With America" was coming to town. It promised lowered deficits, lowered taxes, and lowered services for children, without hurting anyone. It seemed that just as we know we can't write checks we can't cash (or shouldn't at least), Congress was soon to learn it could not (should not) write a contract it couldn't fulfill. And no one was thinking about a contract for children. So I did.

દ્ય

Santa Claus Mentality Means Lump of Coal for Kids

At the risk or sounding like the Grinch Who Stole Christmas, I'm compelled to run counter to our popular cultural assumptions and affirm this holiday season that, in fact, there is no Santa Claus.

All of us from early childhood have been raised to believe in a jolly fat man who brings us gifts by our merely making requests. While this is a wonderful childhood notion, unfortunately, most of us carry it into our adult lives. We somehow grow up believing there are gifts coming without a need to pay for them. Nowhere has this been more obvious than in our recent elections and the polling results from the American public about what they want for their country.

When you listen to what people seem to be saying, they appear to believe they can have it all—lower taxes, better services, no deficit and increased spending for the military. I have yet to uncover an economist who believes all of those things are possible. Economics will not support these countervailing desires; they are an irreconcilable paradox.

It seems clear that with the sea change taking place in Washington, we'll see how promises have a hard time keeping pace with reality. The incoming Congress has made a "Contract With America" that is a clear example of clashing desires. It promises lower taxes and increased spending for the military, while keeping the deficit low.

Incoming congressional leaders, meanwhile, want to move government out of the people's business and at the same time impose a constitutional amendment on school prayer. They're going to put a heavy emphasis on family values, while at the same time reducing financial support for poor children. They're going to cut spending for social programs that might help prevent crime, and move that money into support for prisons.

This desire to have it all without paying a price is not limited to Congress either. Schools have struggled for years with the problems caused by unlimited wants coupled with few responsibilities: Children working after school, overemphasizing athletics and other extracurricular activities, and watching six hours of television a day are not children who are likely to outrank international competitors who do not have the same distractions.

Testing is another good example of wanting two outcomes that are diametrically opposed. We see increased demands in the workplace for higher skilled, more complex thinking workers, yet our short-term-focused desires mean we continue to test our children on rote learning and "rabbit pellet" information processing.

It's time for all of us to realize that we cannot have it all. We have to set priorities.

A good place to start would be a "Contract for America's Children." Some of the planks might be the following:

❧ **No child should be allowed to be hungry, sick or unloved.** In a culture where one child in five is living in poverty, this would be a major first step. We cannot have an economy that competes with the rest of the world and children who compete with the rest of the world when our children come to school hungry, sick and uncared for, if they come at all.

❧ **People doing the work for the nation's children should be affirmed and supported, not trashed and trampled.** People who work with children are the unsung heroes of our culture and deserve far more support and affirmation than they receive.

❧ **Children's success in school should be at the top of the agenda.** Often we're asking schools to do contradictory things. We want to reduce the number of children dropping out; at the same time, we want to give high-stakes tests to children that ensure that a third or fourth of them will not pass and cannot finish or be given a diploma. We need to set one course and then stick with it.

❧ **Money should not be thrown at schools. It should be targeted at specific solutions.** Politicians love to say that we shouldn't be throwing money at problems, as if anyone has ever suggested that. However, looking at specific problems and finding funds to help solve them is a good place to start making things better.

❧ **No politician should be allowed to criticize without a solution, and no false solutions should be offered.** Politicians are fond of coming up with "easy," low-cost solutions to problems that they find painless. The most painless is pointing the finger of blame at someone else. The fact is that most of our problems are much more complex than politicians want to believe and much more difficult to solve than they would like their constituents to believe. We must hold our leaders accountable for their suggestions and for backing up their suggestions with facts.

My humble wish in this holiday season is that we start putting children at the top of our agenda and become a caring nation for our most precious resource. That would be a real gift to one another, Santa or no Santa.

ે

On rare occasions the press says something good about public education. In late 1994, *Money* magazine published an article that pointed out that public schools were as good as private schools. While the article made us feel a bit better, the real issue is whether any comparison of two systems built upon such different assumptions is valid.

ﻬ

Money's Public School Praise
No News to Educators

It's become so rare for a national publication to say anything good about public schools, that when they do, it must be considered news.

That's exactly what happened in the October issue of *Money* magazine. The article by Denise M. Topolnicki trumpeted the fact that public schools are as good as private schools, or at least the better public schools are as good as the better private schools. While this may have been a startling revelation for the readers of *Money*, those of us working in public education weren't surprised.

More shocking was the fact that a national publication finally found some good news to write about public schools. Unfortunately, the tone of the article was critical of private schools—elevating public schools at their expense. Having been on the receiving end of that sort of attitude for a long time, I felt sympathy for private school educators.

The fact is that both public and private schools at the top of the income scale do a good job.

Some findings cited in the *Money* article:

ੴ Students who attend the best public schools outperform most private school students;

ੴ The average public school teacher tends to have stronger academic qualifications than the average private school teacher;

ੴ The best public schools offer more challenging curricula than most private schools;

ੴ Public school class sizes are no larger than those in private schools and are actually smaller than in most Catholic schools; and

ੴ About 30 percent of the kids who live in affluent public school districts attend private schools.

The last finding—that private school attendance in affluent neighborhoods is much higher than the national average—drove the article's author to question the degree to which there is a payoff for private school tuition, given the quality of public high schools in affluent districts.

Peter Relic, who is president of the National Association of Independent Schools, came out with his own response to the *Money* article. He pointed out that the cost of private schooling tends to be much lower than the article led one to believe, with the average tuition cost for day schools at about $8,200.

He also noted that while private schools are indeed selective, about three out of five students who apply are accepted for admission. Obviously, this is not the 100 percent admission rate that public schools have, but perhaps it is higher than many people realize. He also pointed out that private schools have done well in approaching diversity through providing tuition support for needy students. And while public school teachers may have more years of education on average than private school teachers, he noted that most private school teachers have majored in the subjects they teach.

The real bottom line here is that any comparison of public schools and private schools is apples to oranges. It revolves around the fact that public schools are for everybody. Their greatest strength and weakness is that public schools have to accept and educate everyone. Private schools are not for everyone. They do not have to accept everyone, and they can be more selective and focused in their curriculum. I would argue that in a strong democratic society there is a place for both of these.

It is well to consider this as we, as public educators, undoubtedly face a new push for vouchers that would allow students to attend private schools at taxpayer expense. Any policy that mixes public and private education systems will end up weakening both.

The wisdom in the *Money* article is that affluence has a major impact on quality. This is not a shocking finding, but one worth reinforcing. Children who live in affluent communities, whether they go to public school or private school, tend to have a very good education and tend to be set up very nicely for life. Children who go to schools in less affluent communities with less support tend to face many more problems. I think this is something we as a nation should worry about. Despite what our critics might say, money does matter.

Further, rather than pitting public schools and private schools against each other, I think we ought to find ways to work together and to build on each other's strengths. Most importantly, we as a nation need to come to grips with what we do about children who come from poverty, and we must work to find realistic solutions to that instead of the silly solutions, competition and scapegoating that seem to be prevalent in the national press and among our critics.

ક્રે

In early 1995 Congress helped coin a new term—it was the verb "to be school lunched." This term came about because of a proposal to block grant nutrition programs for schools. The outcome would have resulted in a long-term, severe curtailment in school lunch programs. The new Congress came to learn a painful lesson—America does not like folks who overtly do things that will hurt children.

ૐ

Block Grants
Would Starve Nutrition Programs

Two U.S. House committees recently took dramatic steps backward for the health and education of our nation's children.

The U.S. House of Economic and Educational Opportunities Committee voted in February, despite overwhelming opposition from educators, nutritionists and school lunch officials, to dismantle the National School Lunch Act.

Meanwhile, the House Appropriations Committee has slashed $1.7 billion from already funded education programs.

Under the new nutrition block grant, funds from the program would be disbursed to state governors, who could direct up to 20 percent of their block grants to nutrition programs other than school lunch.

The GOP plan also bases a growing percentage of each state's block grant on the number of meals served, regardless of whether those meals are free or reduced-price. That will almost guarantee that poorer states will get less money. High-growth states will suffer as well, since the total block grant to any one state may not grow by more than 4.5 percent per year.

In the past, the committee had treated the lunch program as a nutrition "entitlement," which means all who were eligible were served. The School Lunch Act is not and has never been considered a welfare or poverty program. It provides nutritionally valuable meals to children with rapidly developing minds and bodies in the crucial early years of life, and it provides an outlet for farm commodities when market prices are poor.

Any teacher can tell you that a hungry child simply cannot learn up to his or her ability. Common sense dictates that this program should remain available to all children, with families paying the portion of the cost that they can afford.

This program runs smoothly and efficiently now, both in states and in local school districts. Why tamper with a proven child-oriented program that works?

A House GOP staff member said they "had to make $6 billion in cuts" in the child nutrition programs, apparently to satisfy the leadership's "Contract With America" rhetoric. This zeroing in on nutrition programs for kids is sheer folly. There's no bureaucratic "fat" here, as local school superintendents and school lunch directors know.

Back in 1981, when the infamous Gramm/Latta budget reconciliation bill roared through the House with precious little discussion, the School Lunch Act cuts resulted in 2,000 schools dropping out of the School Lunch Program, and a total of 2 million children no longer received the meals.

Is that what we want as our legacy to our children: less food, less energy, less learning?

And the school lunch proposal is not the only congressional action likely to have dramatically negative consequences for children and their local schools.

As part of its 9.57 percent cut in elementary and secondary education, the Labor, Health and Human Services and Education Appropriations Subcommittee voted to terminate support for educational technology. This at a time when classroom teachers and their students are a long way from being full participants in the information age. A 1994 report from a U.S. Department of Commerce task force estimated that 80 percent of all school computers are obsolete. In addition, only one in seven classrooms has the phone line necessary to connect students via computer networks such as those accessible via Internet, and only 4 percent of teachers have a modem in their classroom, according to a study by the National Education Association.

The committee also voted to kill the Safe and Drug-Free Schools Program. This program was aimed directly at high-poverty areas and was meant to help alleviate violence. Dropping this $481 million program is a travesty for dedicated people trying to bring civility to our nation's streets and even better education to our children.

The committee also terminated the Parents and Teachers Program, cut a portion of the Title I Remedial Reading Program for poor children as well as the evaluation of the program and knocked out programs for dropouts and homeless children and youth.

The subcommittee also decided to wipe out both the 1995 and 1996 Summer Youth Programs, an added loss of $1.73 billion.

Federal education funding has been largely responsible for dramatic strides made in closing the achievement gap during the past 20 years. For black students, test scores rose approximately 40 percent between 1975 and 1990.

Wholesale slashing in Washington will lead to more, not less, inequality. As the tax burden shifts to the local level, let's not forget that the reason the federal government stepped in to fund programs such as compensatory education was because the needs of the poor and disadvantaged were not being met by states and cities.

How can we teach our children to be civil when many of our own elected leaders have decided not to treat them with civility?

Just as schools have learned to survive in new and different times, AASA has also had to learn that same lesson. In addition to writing and speaking on your behalf, I have also had to keep your national organization viable. That called for doing business a different way. Since that period of reinvention in 1995, we have emerged, in many ways, stronger than ever. Once again, a reminder that the strongest steel is tempered in the hottest fires.

ર્≥

Learning To Play Leapfrog in a New World

A friend recently shared with me a picture of a 1938 Packard along with a reminder of why the Packard no longer is on the market. The makers forgot they had a market niche that provided high-quality, high-priced cars to those who wanted them. When the company cheapened its cars to attract the low-price buyers, it died.

What do Packards have to do with school leaders? Everything. A major problem for schools in the last few years has been that we aren't very clear on what we are supposed to be producing. We used to know what our jobs were. We were supposed to process children for a differentiated workplace. We picked the winners and losers, trained them accordingly and provided the workers and managers for a powerful industrial complex.

We are still doing that and we're doing it better than ever—doing a better job of educating 1990s kids for the 1950s. While we make incremental improvements, the needs of children and the expectations of the workplace increase exponentially.

What is needed is a clear statement of a new mission and a willingness on our part to respond to that mission by totally transforming our institutions. Our old task was to preside over a 100-yard dash and give out blue ribbons for first, second and third place. The new mission is to organize a marathon race, which is longer and tougher, and see to it that everyone finishes. We must lead politicians, business partners, parents and communities in discussions designed to achieve consensus about our mission, then get on with it.

But before we do this, we must become more attuned to our surroundings. We must pay attention to what is happening to us.

Many of us are familiar with the story of the complacent frog: The frog, when placed in boiling water, will leap out, but when placed in a pot of water gradually heated to boiling, will happily boil to death.

In American schools, and at AASA, we have become a bunch of boiled frogs. The heat has been turned up on us, and we didn't notice it until we became too warm to deal with it. I would like to think that it is not too late for us to respond to this stimulus by becoming transformational leaders who can reshape our organizations into new places for growth and learning.

We must reinvent ourselves dramatically to remain viable, not because we have done a poor job, as many critics claim, but because we are doing the wrong job.

AASA, like many other institutions, suffers from the Packard/Boiled Frog Syndrome. The American Association of School Administrators, historically, has been a very strong organization that catered to the superintendent of America. We now exist in an international environment that challenges our very name. The demands on educators call for more than mere "association." Our focus must be on learning, not just "schools." And we cannot "administer" our districts to greatness. We must lead them there.

We must broaden our focus beyond our borders; we must look at learning comprehensively, and we must focus on leadership. At the same time, we must concentrate more precisely on the mission of supporting the "superintendency" and system leadership. We want to attract and support all members of the leadership team, with our focus always on children.

AASA has much to do to respond to these new mandates. We have failed to modify our programs and products to keep pace with the superheated environment of the frog. We have not reshaped ourselves into a 21st century organization that models what the new world will look like.

We have recently undergone what I refer to as "right-sizing," downsizing and restructuring our organization as a first step toward being leaner and more responsive. We will be maximizing our resources and focusing on the business that must be conducted.

From my own experience as a superintendent, this is nothing that most school systems haven't already dealt with as a part of doing business. Meanwhile, I expect we'll have a few bumps in the road as we adjust our staffing and roles. I hope you will be patient and supportive as we try to make AASA all that you want it to be and all that it must be to support your critical role. If you have ideas and suggestions, we welcome them.

Meanwhile, if you see a few frogs hopping around with blisters, don't be alarmed. It's your friendly AASA staff trying to find a new way, in a new world.

Some things are certain. The sun always comes up in the East. And you can count on a new report about education to emerge every few days. Most are forgettable. Some laughable. Many are irritating. And a few are worth our attention. One of these was a RAND Corporation report on student achievement that reinforced the fact that schools have not done nearly as badly as the critics would have us believe; in fact, some government programs seem to work. The other report was less upbeat. It was from the Public Agenda Foundation and showed that an immense gap exists between what educators and the public think about schools. Bridging that gap is vital if we are to ever succeed.

ॐ

Use Data, Dialogue
To Correct Perceptions

Two recent reports—one on student achievement, the other on public expectations for schools—arm school leaders with powerful facts about the successes of our schools and what we need to do to ensure their continued viability. The RAND Report on "Student Achievement and the Changing American Family" and "First Things First—What Americans Expect From the Public Schools," from the Public Agenda Foundation, are worthwhile reading.

Basically, the RAND report found that, rather than declining, student math and reading performance improved for all major racial and ethnic groups between 1970 and 1990, as measured by the National Assessment of Educational Progress. Black students made the most dramatic strides, but Hispanic students also registered quite large gains. This finding refutes those who argue that achievement has declined over the past two decades, particularly for minority children. An achievement gap remains, but the last 20 years have seen a decrease in that gap.

A second finding was that rather than being a drag, the changes in family demographics during that time period actually helped boost test scores. The major factor was the rising level of parental education, which has a powerful effect, particularly for black families. The combination of a stable family income and declining family size are also major positive factors, because they increase the amount of resources available for each child.

The third finding was that, rather than being ineffective, the nation's large investment in public education, social programs and equal opportunity policies may be the major contributor to these payoffs in minority achievement. Researchers felt that this was true because the black and Hispanic student test score gains were greater than the changing family characteristics would explain. The best explanation for this is that some school and government efforts are having a positive effect.

Taken together, these three findings fly in the face of some of the negative rhetoric aimed at schools to justify "devolving" control of education through vouchers or otherwise removing federal support. The RAND study buttresses arguments for more support for poor families, rather than less.

We educators have a difficult sell trying to get people to understand that we are doing better than they think we are. The RAND researchers have helped our case immensely. More importantly, the RAND study makes a clear and compelling case for why powerful social policies aimed at children and families have a strong, positive payoff for our nation. We have not merely been throwing money at problems, as our critics might see it.

Meanwhile, the Public Agenda Foundation report, while its outlook about public education is not nearly as positive, deserves our attention. It is based on a series of surveys with Americans telling what they expect from public schools. The problem, very clearly, is that what we think about schools and what our public thinks about us are at odds.

For example, the thing that most Americans believe the schools are not providing, as a minimum prerequisite for education, is a safe and orderly environment and teaching of the basics. While most of us believe that most of our schools fit this bill, it would seem that Americans all across the country believe that we are not providing this basic underpinning for sound education. The study shows that too many Americans are concerned that too many public schools are so disorderly and undisciplined that learning cannot take place. This has been joined by a new fear that the schools are violent and unsafe. Unless we are able to show, through decisive action and through powerful messages, that this is not the case, we will continue to be assaulted by a lack of confidence from the public.

Other findings of the report show that Americans want higher standards and think students should be held accountable for that.

The public is uncomfortable with reforms and innovations, and believes in and wants some educational practices that may be very difficult for educators to stomach. Tracking and the use of multiple-choice tests are among them. The fact is that the public is far more traditional in its view of education than we are. The public wants better schools, but not different ones.

I don't believe that these findings mean that we should abandon the issue of reform or give ourselves over to back-to-basics. But we have to do a much better job of communicating effectively with our public why we are embarking on reforms; explain the reforms clearly, in noneducational jargon; and prove that students are mastering "the basics" at the same time.

The RAND and Public Agenda studies point out both the perils and the possibilities of professional school leadership. Our children's future demands that we herald the successes of our common schools. At the same time, we must listen sincerely to the concerns of our parents and communities, then follow through vigorously on a shared agenda for even greater successes in the next century.

School lunches again! In moving around Washington, I was struck that at a time when children had been placed in the political cross hairs, every politician seemed to be sporting a "Save the Children" tie. I got so worked up I decided to stop wearing mine until those who were hurting kids moved to a new fad and I sat down and wrote this piece. Now that the politicians have stopped wearing the ties, having moved on to other things, I once again wear mine with pride.

ॐ

Dear Congress:
Can the Ties; Save the Children

Washington is a place known more for style than substance. Therefore, it is important to take note when the style changes.

Lately, we've seen a sharp increase in the number of politicians wearing "Save the Children" neckties. That's a sure sign that our kids are about to get chopped up once more in the political process. No sooner had the tags been taken off the ties than the new budget proposal passed the House in late May, calling for a reduction of some $68 billion (yes, that's billion with a B) going to education over the next seven years.

If that is not bad enough, these reductions have been cynically packaged by the majority party as a way of ensuring our children's future by reducing the federal deficit. Certainly, we don't want to pass on that kind of problem to our children. However, we also must recognize that by demolishing the national role in education through these draconian reductions, we are creating a more serious problem: failing to address the inequities and basic need for investment in our children. That has been the historic federal role.

If you closely examine the byproducts of the work of Congress, it is not merely an attempt to make the tough budget-cutting decisions to ensure our children's future that supporters of the cuts claim. If they were making an honest attempt to share the burden of deficit reduction across the whole spectrum of government spending, I would still argue that the poorest and most vulnerable of our nation, our children, should be spared. But, at least I could buy the claims of the politicians that they are trying to do a tough job fairly. What I find so outrageous is that, in fact, the children have been placed at the head of the line for punishment, and that the social policy being pursued by the Congress exacerbates and accelerates the recent trend of separating our nation into two parts: one poor, the other rich. It is neither enlightened nor fair.

Let's look at the school lunch reductions as an example. There have been all sorts of arguments about whether the proposals were reductions in spending or in projected increases. The fact is, the way the formulas were devised, it all depends on where you live. There are 55 states and territories affected by the allocations. Only 10 will receive increased funding, by a total of $65.6 million. However, of the 45 that will lose funding, the 10 that will lose the most will lose more than a billion dollars over the next few years. But that doesn't begin to tell the story.

If you look at the 10 wealthiest states (and for the purposes of this analysis we will define "wealthy" as those states having the smallest percentage of students in poverty) you find that over the next five years those 10 states together will lose a total of $5 million in funding for the school lunch program. It's a loss, but a modest one. However, the 10 poorest states (those with the greatest percentage of children in poverty) will lose $857 million over the next five years—a staggering amount for children who are already at risk because of family poverty.

Clearly, this Congress has shaped a social policy that reduces the deficit by rewarding the rich and punishing the poor. If the story stopped there, it would be bad enough. But it doesn't stop there.

Former Education Secretary William Bennett, the outspoken and acerbic critic of public educators who now heads the conservative think tank Empower America, has devised a "Report Card on America's Schools" that shows some states do better than others at educating children, at least by his definition, which includes having relatively high SAT scores compared with per-pupil expenditures. His premise is that money doesn't matter, and that you can have good results without financial support.

Bennett's top 10 states share one common quality. They are states that are very modestly impacted by the grinding social factors that make educating children difficult. Bennett's 10 states tend to have small percentages of children in poverty, from single- and teen-parent families and whose native language is not English. One would expect that because they have less need, these 10 states might not fare well when the federal budget is being reduced to curb the deficit. Not so. These 10 states will get $42.47 million more for their school lunch programs over the next five years.

A similar analysis of the recent reading report card from the National Assessment of Educational Progress is also instructive. The report pointed out that 8 states showed solid progress while 10 other states declined. How did they do with lunch funding, since hungry children might not concentrate or read as well as their well-fed peers? The 10 states that showed declines in reading will average a $16 million loss per state over the next five years. The eight states that improved will average $17 million in increases during the same period.

So the rich get richer and the poor get poorer. Those who are doing well get the support, and those who are not doing so well get punished. Perhaps some feel this is appropriate: that a merit system is what America is about. But no one in Congress has suggested they meant to create a lunch program formula that awards dollars based on academic success, though that is the result.

The future of our nation is at risk because of the gaping disunion between families that can provide for their children and those that cannot. If we fail to use the collective power of our country to address the needs of poor children, it will take more than a tie to save them.

೭ৱ

More high jinks from Washington, D.C. This column appeared amidst much talk of doing away with the Department of Education. While I am a fan of U.S. Secretary Richard Riley, I am not enamored with the department. However, the issue is not about bureaucracy nearly as much as it is about what we deem important enough to have the president's ear.

಄

If Not Education, How About a Children's Department?

The current Congress is so busy putting forth their new ideas for America that it takes a score card to keep up with them. One of the more disappointing is a proposal to eliminate the Department of Education. This is supposed to save money, reduce bureaucracy, and return power to the states. It is based on the premise that education is not mentioned in the Constitution: therefore it belongs to the states. It is also based on a belief that the Department of Education is a bureaucracy created for the benefit of the professional education establishment.

Ironically, two former education secretaries—William Bennett and Lamar Alexander—are among those conservatives calling for the department to be dismantled. Also an irony, those calling for its demise agree that its main functions should remain part of the federal agenda: aid for disadvantaged and disabled students, loans, statistics, data gathering and research, the bully pulpit.

Federal programs such as Title I will have to be administered by someone. Furthermore, the department spends only about 2 percent of its budget on administration, among the lowest administrative overhead for cabinet agencies. It also has the smallest ratio of employees to budget of any department. Little would be saved by doing away with it, and potentially, much could be lost, including a national focus on education reform at a time of increasing global competitiveness and growing need among our nation's children.

Although the average proportion of school budgets coming from the federal government is only about 6 percent, it is a critical funding source for those struggling to educate the growing number of disadvantaged students. It has helped to close the achievement gap, despite the fact that within states large inequities still remain in school district spending. More than 10 percent of the budgets of districts with high concentrations of poor children comes from federal sources.

Recent polls indicate that 77 percent of the public opposes doing away with the department.

Whether any of these arguments prove to be anything more than a speedbump to the congressional juggernaut is questionable. It could be that only a presidential veto will stand in the way of education being downgraded and swallowed by other departments.

But an argument about whether or not to dispense with the Department of Education is clouding a more fundamental issue. I am deeply troubled that in a city where other competing interests would have the president's ear, there would be no voice for children. They may make up 0 percent of our electorate, but they are 100 percent of this country's future. Should they not have a secretary who looks out for them as much as labor, commerce or agriculture?

On a talk show recently, the moderator asked me to explain how two former secretaries of education could propose dismantling the very department they had headed. I replied that if all the education secretaries had been as ineffective in speaking out for children as Bennett and Alexander, I would agree with them. Both of these folks spent most of their time bad-mouthing public schools and the professionals who work in them and trying to dismantle the common school through vouchers, turning children over to the forces of the marketplace.

Fortunately, we have had secretaries like Richard Riley and Terrell Bell, who have used the bully pulpit for the betterment of children, by pointing out the needs of schools and affirming those who do the hard work of supporting them.

The need for a bully pulpit on behalf of children is greater than ever. The issue is, who will speak for them at the national level?

Perhaps we are approaching a time to think more broadly than simply fighting for a Department of Education. Perhaps it is time for a Department for Children. Our founding fathers talked about the rights of our citizens to life, liberty, and the pursuit of happiness — rights that are being denied many of our youngest citizens because of poor health, poverty and a lack of love, caring and support. There is a national purpose for protecting our most vulnerable citizens. There is a national purpose for protecting our nation's future through supporting its children.

A Department for Children should be part of a broad national strategy for supporting children, including funding the first national goal: that all children should come to school ready to learn. For a number of years, AASA has been calling for an investment trust fund for children. We, as educators, must look at the issue of children more broadly and reach out to all groups who support and nurture them. A children's department could help us do that by coordinating programs found not only in the Education Department, but in Labor, Health and Human Services, Agriculture, Defense and the Interior.

The problem is not that the Department of Education is too big. Maybe it, and our thinking about it, is not big enough.

Coordinating services are hailed as the solution to the problems of children and families at the local level. It is time that we recognize the need for building a village around the child at the national level as well. In our concern about international competition, we have overlooked the fact that Germany, Denmark and France all have developed Departments for Children, Youth and Families.

Isn't it time that we ensure a voice for the most voiceless among us?

Some of my columns spring from the moment. Others are spurred by my sense of right or wrong or even some perceived momentary injustice. And a few bubble around in my soul for a long time before I can put my thoughts into words. This column was one of those. It came from way down inside and spoke to what I consider to be America's most troubling issue: racism.

ॐ

Racism: Deadly Disease for the American Dream

America has always been a country at war with itself. Our most profound wars have been our cultural wars—the ones fought for the soul of our nation. We are, at once, the most generous nation to ever have existed, and the most selfish. We are the most inclusive society that the world has ever known; at the same time we have become the most exclusive in our attitudes toward others.

Lately, it seems the selfish side has pulled ahead of the more generous side. I recently told a group of visiting educators from the Netherlands that America is the most Darwinian country ever. We really do believe in the survival of the fittest. We celebrate winners and have little time for losers. This competitive streak has enabled us to become the richest and most powerful country in the world. But we have also come to accept, as a given, great poverty among our citizens.

Our selfishness has narrowed our circle of interest to include a smaller and smaller band. Nowhere is that circle more tightly drawn or uglier than when we deal with race. We are not very happy helping anyone unless they look and act a lot like us. Our selfishness has given rise to a new breed of racism in this country that has the potential to destroy us all.

I believe our old definition of racism, formed in the last century and defined by the first half of this century, has largely, like some terrible disease such as polio, been conquered. We inoculated ourselves against it through massive legal and policy efforts, and the shots worked. However, what has happened is that the disease has mutated like the new "super" viruses that are immune to traditional antibiotics, and the old remedies that used to cure, no longer do. Today's racism is selfishness, driven by fear and a lack of trust, and manifested through economic imperatives. The old racism was a creation of the mind; the new racism is a disease of the heart and pocketbook.

Let's just look around. Within the last year we have seen Proposition 187 pass in California. It would deny health care and education to undocumented aliens. California has been impacted by a tidal wave of immigration, and the federal government has not slowed it down or covered the increased costs for handling these folks. But when you strip away the economics, you find that the long-term costs of dealing with literally millions of people who are in poor health and who have not been educated will dwarf the short-term costs of providing them with basic necessities. There must be something else driving the anti-immigrant mentality. If these new immigrants had been the "right" color or spoken the "right" language, I doubt Prop 187 would have passed.

This past year also saw the publication of *The Bell Curve*, which purports to prove what some folks have always believed—that some races are smarter than others. The book, by Richard J. Herrnstein and Charles A. Murray, suggests that America is being divided between cognitive "haves" and "have nots." It argues that the country is run by a cognitive group of "elites" who are isolated from a large and growing underclass that is far less intelligent. The most problematic part of the book is the authors' contention that blacks as a group are intellectually inferior to whites, and that there is not much that education, or intervention of any sort, can do to close the gap.

The publication and general acceptance of a book like *The Bell Curve* demonstrates that the pendulum has swung to a place where we have decided that it is open season on those who are different than we are. However, we need to look closely at what this means. America is becoming a more diverse country and a country in which the very definition of race and color is becoming less meaningful. Demographer Harold Hodgkinson points out that if you go back five generations, 80 percent of all Americans are of some mixed race. What then does race really mean? He also reports a study that indicated that, as measured by a light meter, the darkest of white Americans are darker than the lightest of African Americans. What then, does color mean?

What is driving our current obsession with race is an economy and social system that has tightened the circle around the American Dream. In an article by Stanley Greenberg, President Clinton's pollster, which appeared in *Michigan Monthly*, the rising sense of racism is tied to the declining fortunes of the white middle class. Greenberg found that, as a group, they professed a profound distaste for black Americans—"a sentiment that pervaded almost everything they thought about government and politics."

"Blacks constituted the explanation for their vulnerability and for almost everything that had gone wrong in their lives; not being black was what constituted being middle class; not having blacks was what made a neighborhood a decent place to live." Greenberg's study also found that the whites he talked to "rejected out of hand the social justice claims of black Americans. They denied that blacks suffer special disadvantages that would require special treatment by employers or government. They had no historical memory of racism and no tolerance for present efforts to offset it."

This mentality is what has fed the militia movement that we have read so much about in recent months. We have created a whole substrata of our nation that does not merely distrust its government, but has come to hate it. They feel totally left out of the possibilities of our nation and estranged from the American Dream. The irony is that now we have blacks and whites who both feel that we have government that conspires against its citizens.

In this context, we see part of Herrnstein and Murray's intellectual elite, the Congress, taking food from hungry children to feed capital gains tax breaks to the wealthy. We see elected representatives who decry violence in the media and line up to protect the rights of those who want to preserve assault weapons. It is easy to see why our citizens are cynical about their government.

We are rushing headlong as a nation toward a precipice. On one side, we are gathering a larger and larger portion of our population who feel that they are being closed off from the American Dream because of their color, language or national origin. On the other side, we have the angry white middle class who see their hold on the dream becoming more and more tenuous. A couple of years ago we saw, in the L.A. riots, what can happen when a sense of exclusion festers into despair. Recently we apparently saw, in the Oklahoma City bombing, what can happen when angry white men pull completely away from their roots in a civil society. What we are facing as a nation is nothing less profound than the potential of a revolution between two sides of the political spectrum. This racial squeeze play does not bode well for our nation.

As we look at where our country is going, and whether our lighter nature of trust and generosity will overcome our darker nature of fear and selfishness, we should recall what the poet John Donne said, and ask not for whom the bell curves; it curves for thee. We must find a way to turn the curve on its head and move upward on the arc toward a society that gives hope to its people and to a world that includes, and says yes to, the dreamer in each of us.

ॐ

More dopiness from D.C. Congress was busily cutting money for schools. Meanwhile, it was trying to create tax cuts for the wealthy. This led me, as an old school person, to only one logical suggestion . . .

૨&

A Car Wash To Offset a Waxing in Congress

There is an old joke about two guys. One is depressed. The other tells him to cheer up, things could get worse. So he cheered up, and sure enough, things got worse. I thought of this as I surveyed the wreckage that this Congress has recently made of educational policy and funding. We are witnessing a collision between the escalating needs of a significant portion of our children and the incredibly insensitive and callous actions of a majority of our elected representatives. It's a tough way to start the school year.

What the House did this summer was cut education spending by 17.2 percent, a whopping $4.4 billion. In the same budget, Congress reduced Health and Labor spending by smaller numbers. House members claimed to be protecting our children from a terrible national debt. Unfortunately, that is a bogus claim. These cuts fail the fairness test.

In reality, the "deficit busters" managed to increase defense spending by more than $7 billion above what the Pentagon requested. The House has chosen to fund missile and bomber programs the military didn't even ask for, at a time when we have no declared enemies and when the United States already spends more than *twice* as much as our combined potential enemies do on military operations.

Education was singled out for more severe treatment, and, once again, poor kids are the big losers. More than a quarter of the education reductions came from Title I, and much of the rest came from Dropout Prevention and Safe and Drug-Free Schools money.

But wait . . . cheer up . . . it gets worse! Congress is in the process of revamping vocational education. This comes under the heading of "The School Leader's Worst Nightmare" because, while school administrators still will be held accountable for program results as funds are reduced, others in the community, such as representatives from business, will have broad powers to design the delivery system for vocational education. You will have fewer resources that someone else will decide how to spend, and you will get the blame if programs don't work out.

There is some positive news. Through the work of AASA staff members, magnet schools grants were exempted from a mega-block grant that merged 50 separate programs and cut funding for them in half. Of less comfort, Chapter 2 and staff development funds were among those consolidated into the smaller pot of money. Now governors will decide how to spend it.

Meanwhile, reauthorization of special education is working its way through Congress. The good new is that Congress appears willing to address the troubling issue of discipline. The news is you'll likely have even less money to address the needs, and again, the governors will get control, which introduces the specter of politics dictating which disabilities get the most help.

What can you do? There are a few possibilities. This month, the Committee for Education Funding, a coalition of 100 education groups including AASA, will hold a national bake sale on the lawn of the Capitol, where cookies will be sold for $1,000 each. Local communities are encouraged to do the same.

In like-minded spirit, AASA is considering having a car wash to raise money for schools. We figure that if we charge $2,000 apiece, we'd only have to wash 500,000 cars to offset the cuts. We'll follow the lead of Congress, which will use money saved from education to offer tax breaks for the wealthiest Americans: We'll offer price breaks for limos by increasing the price for a compact car wash. We know federal lawmakers will be the first in line, since they believe so strongly in local action and self-help.

I offer the preceding suggestions only partly in jest. The fact is that we must find ways to bring education funding to the top of the national agenda. So far, we cannot count on the Senate to undo House members' misdeeds. Senators are talking of "softening" the cuts from 17 percent to 15 percent. And although President Clinton is threatening a veto, the last time he vetoed such cuts — in the fiscal 1995 recession package — he later signed a bill that still left most of the reductions intact.

If things are to get better, it will be through the independent and collective action of local leaders, like yourselves, across the country. You have a powerful voice in your community. You can bring the plight of your children to your community's attention and dramatize the effects of education funding cuts on your children. The time to act is now.

This Congress thinks they were sent to Washington to slash spending. I believe they have missed the mandate. I believe Americans care about our children. They have no interest in seeing mean-spirited leadership, which targets children as a liability. I've had the opportunity to testify before this Congress. Some of them make Jack the Ripper look like Barney the dinosaur. They need their chains pulled by their constituents, and you can start the process. Only then will things really get better, and then maybe we could really cheer up.

One frustration for school leaders is the story told about schools by the popular press. When they don't get it wrong, they often miss the point. In writing about the *Condition of Education Report of 1995* the news media missed the point. I thought somebody had to set the record straight.

ﻉﻪ

Not the Whole Story, But a True Story Nonetheless

Fall has always been a time when educators dig down and put all their energy into starting a new school year. Over the last few years, we have also had to hunker down in a self-protective stance as we faced the latest barrage of reports telling the American people how lousy their schools are and how much worse they have gotten since last year. A funny thing happened this fall: The reports show things are getting better. We in education hardly know how to react—and neither do our critics.

Over the past few weeks we have heard from the College Board that SAT scores are up, and from the American College Testing service that scores on the ACT are stable, despite an increasing pool of test takers. We have seen the Department of Education issue its "Condition of Education" report showing that kids are taking tougher courses in record numbers; the number of dropouts is down; and the achievement gap between majority and minority kids is closing. In fact, as the late Howard Cosell might say, we've been subjected to a veritable plethora of good news.

Let's put all this into context. The reality is that most indicators have been on a steady upward trend since the early 1980s. It seems some of the media have just awakened to the fact. Also, this year's gains were a bit more dramatic than the other incremental bumps, so it appears more newsworthy. Further, we have a Secretary of Education, Richard Riley, who prefers to accentuate the positive, in contrast to some of his predecessors who seemed to delight in trashing public education.

There have been some interesting responses to all of this. First, some of the media seem too shocked to comment. Others find it too difficult to change their approach so they continue to put a negative spin on a positive story. One AASA member sent me a clipping that heralded the "Condition of Education" report (which is the most comprehensive report issued by the Department of Education annually) by sticking it on page eight and covering it in three paragraphs with the headline "Education gap remains between blacks, whites." What the report really pointed out was that there is a long-standing gap that has narrowed. On the SAT, for example, most ethnic groups have experience larger score gains since 1987, on average, than white students.

What did the press miss? Among the many findings of the "Condition of Education" report were:

1. High school students are taking harder courses, especially in math and science. Between 1982 and 1992 the percentage of high school graduates taking the core courses recommended in "A Nation at Risk" increased sharply from 13 to 47 percent. More students are taking algebra, geometry, trigonometry and calculus.

2. Math and science proficiency have increased. Between 1982 and 1992 the math and science proficiency scores of 17-year-olds on the

National Assessment of Educational Progress (NAEP) increased 9 and 11 points, respectively, on each assessment. This is roughly equivalent to an additional year of learning in high school.

3. More high school graduates go to college immediately after high school, even though college costs continue to rise relative to family income. Between 1980 and 1993 the proportion of high school graduates going directly to college increased from 49 to 62 percent. Most of these were four-year colleges and universities. At the same time, costs increased from 10 percent to 14 percent of median family income.

4. The U.S. population compares favorably with other countries with regard to educational attainment. Eighty-seven percent of 25- to 34-year-olds have completed high school in the United States. This figure is higher than other developed countries except for Germany and Japan (86.5 percent in the United States compared with 90.6 percent in Japan and 88.6 percent in Germany). A significantly higher proportion of Americans have completed a B. A. degree than in other developed countries, except for Japan, which lags slightly behind the United States (23.6 percent to 22.9 percent). Significantly, a much higher percentage of young women have completed higher education in the United States compared with other countries (23 percent in the United States compared with 12 percent in Japan and 11 percent in Germany).

5. There are positive economic returns from education. More high school graduates are employed than non-graduates (64 percent to 47 percent). Earnings are also greater for those employed. The gap in earnings between college graduates and high school graduates has widened since the early 1980s.

Perhaps the most interesting response to all this good news has been from the critics of education (that gang of "nattering nabobs of negativism," to quote a former vice president) who have been pounding away at education for its failings over the past two decades. One might assume that all this positive data would be welcomed. You might even think they would celebrate our awakening to their cause. *Au contraire.* I have appeared on national TV shows in the past several weeks with some of these people. What have I heard? That the data are being misinterpreted in an attempt to save the election of the president, preserve the Department of Education and/or stop vouchers. I have also heard that there is more to the story than data, or that getting better isn't good enough.

With the preponderance of evidence coming from so many places, not just the Department of Education, it would appear that regardless of people's motivations in using the data, the story of improvement is pretty clear. Also, it is almost humorous to see people who have used negative data for years to prove how badly we are doing, suddenly begin questioning whether the data are reliable and whether they should be used at all.

It is true that learning is much more complex than our tools have the ability to measure and that data must be weighed within a broader context. No, these recent statistics are not the whole story. But no one can deny that schools are doing better on those limited things we can measure.

Critics are also right to point out that doing better is not good enough. We need to continue our efforts at improvement. We even need to find new ways of educating children because of the rapid deterioration in their social conditions and changed expectations in the work world. We certainly need to find ways to continue narrowing the gaps in achievement among groups of our children, not simply so that we can wave around statistics, but so that we can open the American Dream to everyone.

However, it doesn't hurt to occasionally pause in our pilgrimage to reflect on how far we have come and to drink a bit from the fountain of success before continuing our journey toward a better education for all our children.

ès

One problem I always faced as an active administrator was never having enough time to read everything I should. I used to depend on friends to suggest what books were worthy of my limited reading time. Now, I try to return the favor from time to time. In this column, I mentioned two books that are still must-reads for school leaders (which, by the way, are available through AASA). One arms us with facts, and the other reminds us why we do battle. (Both, by the way, are now available from AASA's Distribution Center 1-888-782-2272.)

ॐ

Information, Inspiration: Must-Reads for Leaders

One of the challenges of leadership is to constantly "refill the well" of information and inspiration. Throughout the course of the day, people come to you for solutions and information. If you do not replenish yourself, you end up with an intellectual and psychological deficit. This month I'd like to offer two book suggestions that I feel are "must-reads" for educational leaders. The first gives us a better sense of how to fight the battle; the second is a powerful reminder of why we fight the battles we do.

Authors David Berliner and Bruce Biddle have written what I consider the final rebuttal to the critics of America's public schools: *The Manufactured Crisis: Myths, Frauds, and the Attack on America's Public*

Schools. In many ways this book is a culmination of the work started by Sandia National Laboratory researchers in the *Sandia Report*; by AASA Deputy Executive Director Joe Schneider and me in *Exploding the Myths*; and by Gerald Bracey, executive director of the Alliance for Curriculum Reform, in *Transforming America's Schools.*

What Berliner and Biddle have done is close the loop completely and powerfully. They are two of America's most outstanding researchers, and their work is unassailable. They give us a great toolbox to use in fighting the good fight. *The Manufactured Crisis* is a comprehensive, yet very readable book that covers the attacks on schools, rebuts them and tells who is behind the attacks and why. It provides an overview of the real problems confronting education and what might be done about them. The book discusses and debunks the data critics use to make their case: that money doesn't matter and that we are falling behind other countries.

Berliner and Biddle admit that theirs is an angry book. With good reason. Public schools have been under attack by people who should know better. When people recognize the danger to our society created by these attacks—including potential destruction of our school systems—they are bound to get angry. As long as we focus on the wrong set of problems and ignore the real dangers and crises confronting our society and our schools, the real problems will continue to grow and fester.

If *The Manufactured Crisis* makes readers angry, the latest book from Jonathan Kozol will make us ballistic. Kozol has come to be known as the conscience of America when it comes to valuing our children. His earlier works, *Death at an Early Age* and *Savage Inequalities*, spoke with passion and eloquence about those our society leaves behind. I found his new book, *Amazing Grace: The Lives of Children and the Conscience of a Nation*, to be one of the most powerful and moving books I have ever read.

Kozol spent a year talking with and observing the children of the South Bronx in New York City. He uses their voices and their perceptions to paint a horrific portrait of how we treat our children in this country. It is easy to disregard a work based in the ghettos of our largest cities if one happens to live elsewhere; however, the universal truths about our society—its separation of haves from have-nots and its failure to value the one commodity that we all share, our children, are hard to ignore. Kozol puts them before us as a moral issue.

We live in a country where there is a renewal of spirit, at least at the rhetorical level. How then can we sit by as thousands of children die of disease and neglect? Kozol uses the words of the children to hold us all accountable, and the hope of the book is found in the faith of the children.

At one point he quotes a teen-ager whose head is shaved. The kids call that haircut the "25-years-to-life" cut. His sister asks him, "Like in prison? This is how you want to wear your hair?" Her brother replies, "You don't have to be in jail to be in prison." It reminds us that when our children feel like prisoners, we are all their jailers.

Kozol also quotes Anthony, a 13-year-old who speaks of heaven. "No violence will there be in heaven, no guns or drugs or IRS. If you feel lonely in your heart, or bitterness, you'll know you're not there . . . No one will look at you from the outside. People will see you from the inside. All the people from the street will be there. You'll recognize all the children who have died when they were little. God will be there. He'll be happy that we have arrived."

Further into the book Kozol writes of the kindness that the children show animals and strangers. "They show us something very different from the customary picture we are given of a generation of young thugs and future whores. There is a golden moment here that our society has chosen not to seize. We have not nourished this part of the hearts of children, not in New York, not really anywhere," he says.

One of the adults in the community reminds us of what children are. "They are God's spies on earth. His specialized creation . . . I call them spies because they are so vigilant and so observant. They measure us constantly. They try to find out what the hell we think of them."

If this is true, the reports back to heaven on how we are treating God's children are not so good. Kozol puts our moral responsibility before us more powerfully and more honestly than a truckload of televangelists. To be reminded that on this earth, God's work must truly be our own, read *Amazing Grace*.

Better still, invest in some copies of *The Manufactured Crisis* and *Amazing Grace* to distribute to local business and community leaders. It is time we started preaching to the unconverted.

ॐ

While the media focuses people's attention on schools in our urban centers, much can be learned from quieter and gentler areas in rural America. A trip to the back country of Alaska reminded me of some of rural education's virtues and lessons.

እ⤜

Rural Schools:
Creating Education's Future

R ecently, I had the good fortune to visit with our Alaskan affiliate at their annual meeting in King Salmon, Alaska. Aside from enjoying the camaraderie and scenery of what has to be one of the world's most beautiful spots, inhabited by some of the world's most hospitable folks, I came away from the experience with a renewed respect for those in our profession who work in rural America.

Because I am a product of rural America, I have always harbored warm thoughts and feelings for rural education. My professional experience pulled me toward the suburbs and the cities, and I had lost track of the meaning of rural education. One of the experiences I had in Alaska was visiting several of the Eskimo villages that dot the bush of that vast state.

I had the pleasure of meeting dedicated administrators and teachers and experiencing what a K-12 school with 80 children looks like. And, you know what? It looks pretty special. In fact, it looks a lot like what the futurists tell us schools of the future should look like.

There is the old notion that necessity is the mother of invention. When you are running very small schools in an increasingly complicated world, invention is called forth. In many ways, rural education is inventing the future for us.

There are five elements in rural schools that all educators could, and should, be incorporating into their work.

1. Schools as community centers: There is much said today of the need for schools to be the centerpieces of our communities. In fact, I have suggested that we in education, rather than depending on the village to raise the child, must be about the business of building the village. In rural America, the village has been kept alive by the schools that serve as the focal point and service center for the community. Schools open early and stay open late. Often, they are the source of most of the social services for the community. They are the source of entertainment and health, as well as education. Schools in rural America are the centerpiece of the community.

2. Use of technology: While many districts struggle to find the proper use of technology and try to make cases for its support among constituents, rural schools are relying upon it as a basic tool to bring the world into the school and to connect the school to the broader world. Rural schools are avid users of satellite technology for distance learning to ensure that schools with limited numbers do not provide a limited curriculum. Rural schools use the Internet and other computer technology to connect students and to provide them with a richness of resources that would otherwise be prohibited. Technology is not just an enrichment. It is a vehicle for learning.

3. Interdisciplinary instruction: Far too often suburban and urban schools struggle to convince staff and community that the lines between subjects must be broken down because these artificial distinctions are not the way the world is organized or the way learning takes place. Small rural schools must do interdisciplinary instruction simply because there are so few folks to teach the children. They can use this stumbling block as a stepping stone to a more realistic, and in many cases richer, educational experience.

4. Creative scheduling: While many schools are trying to implement block scheduling, the Copernican plan or what have you, many rural schools are just out there doing it because of necessity. It's the only way the kids can get a full curriculum. For example, in Alaska, science teachers are sometimes flown in for extended blocks of time and then moved on to someplace else. The result is that kids can concentrate on the subject and really delve into it.

5. Personalized instruction: School reformers such as Ted Sizer and Debbie Meier have built a persuasive case that, when it come to schooling, small is better. Smaller schools allow a more personalized approach to learning. Students are the center of the action. They can't fall through the cracks unnoticed. The center of the educational universe ought to be the student. In smaller settings the odds are greater; that is the truth.

I don't want to wax too much about rural schools. They face the challenges of limited resources, isolation and fragmentation. But they have made virtues out of some of the problems they have had to confront, and all of us can learn from their creativity and invention.

In one of the villages I visited, I noticed that the school sat right next to the village cemetery, giving new meaning to "womb-to-tomb" education. That juxtaposition also provided a metaphor for the dangers we face if we fail to change our schools to be more creative and more personalized. Unless we become more inventive in creating new solutions to the challenges confronting us, we just might be moved from where we are now to the graveyard of lost opportunities that lies just past the playground next door.

Creating schools for the next century requires not just resources, but also imagination and a real penchant for problem solving. Let's tip our hats to rural America for showing the way.

≥●

Schools and school leaders are forever in the middle of some battle or another. During the mid-'90s one of those battles involved conservatives and liberals. Both sides were right and wrong. Our task is to learn from both, take what's best, and fight the rest, which weakens public schools and undermines the cause of children. And, most of all, we must build bridges so a meeting of the minds is possible. We work in a context where differences will certainly always exist between people— our task is to help folks walk across the bridge to find a common understanding.

ஃ

Ideological War Threatens Children

L ately, I feel more and more like a foreign correspondent observing a war, except that the war I am covering is right here in our nation's capital and the battle is a battle of competing views of America. This battle is being played out in the federal budget discussions. Battles of ideology are interesting and should not be dangerous. However, the outcome of the budget wars of 1995-96 is potentially dangerous because it may have a tremendous impact on the future of children in this country.

Interestingly enough, even the politicians in the trenches understand this at some primitive level. Both sides hold high the banner of children as they wage their verbal jousts. On the one side stand the "liberals" who decry the impact of budget cuts on children and families. They talk about America abandoning its responsibilities to be a fair and caring nation. On the other side are the "conservatives," who say that reaching a balanced budget is critical to the future of our children. Otherwise, they say we will be passing on a ruined economy and a crushing legacy of debt to our children. The irony in this battle is that both sides are right — and wrong.

The conservatives are right in that we need to stop the national penchant for spending large amounts of money we don't have. It is leading us to financial ruin. There are two ways to deal with this. One is to raise revenue (otherwise known as taxes, but it is never called taxes unless it is tied to the word "cut" or you are using it as an adjective to describe an opponent, as in "tax-and-spend liberal"). The other is to reduce spending. Then the question becomes "what to cut?" That is where much of the battle has been fought thus far.

Conservatives have targeted domestic programs for reduction while reducing taxes and increasing military spending. Liberals have proposed reducing military spending, not cutting taxes, and protecting domestic programs. They have loudly decried the proposed impact of cuts in Medicare and Medicaid. Neither side wants to touch Social Security. At the risk of getting shot at from both sides, I would suggest a heretical notion. Perhaps we should raise taxes and cut spending.

How could I possibly suggest raising taxes? You are probably thinking that all that airplane food I've eaten since taking this job has caused brain damage. But the fact is America's tax system is really not up to "world-class standards." Some facts: In the United States our federal, state and local taxes make up 30 percent of our Gross Domestic Product. That is the lowest percentage of any industrialized nation. For example, Germany, a country that we are told we should emulate educationally, gives up 39 percent of its GDP to taxes. England gives up 36 percent. Currently, corporate taxes account for only 2 percent of the GDP. During the Eisenhower administration in the 1950s, considered by many as the golden years of the U.S. economy, business taxes accounted for 5 percent of the GDP.

Despite what we all feel around April 15 each year, the United States is not an overtaxed country and the economy would not suffer if taxes were modestly increased. And we have certainly not overtaxed our wealthiest citizens. Taxes on the wealthy have not leveled wealth. In fact, during the past few decades, the wealthy have gotten wealthier and the poor poorer. Today, America has the greatest income disparity between the "haves" and "have nots" of any developed country. Since education can be a great equalizer, it is not surprising that people would be willing to pay more taxes to improve education. Poll after poll has supported this.

When it comes to how we spend our tax dollars, we could take some lessons from other nations. We spend a larger portion of our budget on the military than other countries, at a time when we have no great enemy with which to contend. But when it comes to helping our children, we are not "world class."

For example, a study conducted for the National Science Foundation found that 25.7 percent of children in the United States are poor. After we apply our tax transfer system (using tax dollars to offset poverty through subsidies and programs) 21.5 percent of children still are living in poverty. Other developed nations do not show this pattern. Of the 17 developed nations in the study, only Ireland (with 30.2 percent of its children living in poverty) and the United Kingdom (with 29.6 percent) start with a larger percentage of children in poverty. Two others, Finland (25.4 percent) and Canada (22.5 percent) have child poverty levels above 20 percent. When tax transfers are applied, a different story emerges. Ireland's child poverty rate drops to 12 percent; the U.K.'s to 9.9 percent; Finland's to 6.5 percent and Canada's to 13.5 percent. Others just do better at addressing the problem.

Conservatives are correct when they point the need to rein in entitlement spending, such as Social Security and Medicare. But no one can argue that these programs, aimed at ending poverty among the elderly, have not worked. The elderly are no longer the poorest segment of our population. Conservatives also are right when they accuse the liberals of demagoguery on this issue. While it is a political hot potato, ignoring the problem of soaring entitlement costs will only saddle our children and grandchildren with another impossible financial burden in the future.

On the other hand, liberals are right to accuse the conservatives of being cold hearted in the way they have approached reducing the deficit. Children have been singled out to bear much of the reduction, even though, as I have pointed out, they already are the poorest segment of our society. Perhaps this is because we are the only industrialized nation without a children's policy. This means every battle is a political one and children have no lobby and no vote. This has led to proposals to cut $7 billion from child nutrition programs, $4 billion from foster and adoption care, reduce Aid to Families with Dependent Children and strip $17 billion from education.

Both sides in this battle need to come together around the real needs of children and stop using them as cannon fodder in an ideological war. Giving children a future unencumbered by staggering debt, which allows them to look forward with optimism, is critical. But so is investing in them now, by providing a safe, healthy and nurturing environment. We cannot ensure our nation's future by robbing children of their present. Everyone must work to ensure that that does not happen.

AASA has to fight for the resources school leaders need to get the job done. Sometimes school folks mistakenly believe that the only battleground is in their immediate vicinity and wonder why AASA fights so hard for federal dollars. They point out that these funds are only a small part of the district budget pie, which is often true. But for many districts, federal dollars represent real meat and potatoes. And be careful of that bureaucrat you criticize . . .

જ⁀

More Needs,
Fewer Federal Dollars for Schools

Some of our members in gentle (and sometimes not so gentle) ways have asked me why in the world AASA is fighting so hard for continued federal funding of education? After all, shouldn't we be for downsizing the federal government and passing more power back to the states? Shouldn't we be for reducing the tax burden on our citizens? Why are we trying to protect the federal share of education spending when it is such a small percentage of education spending? Don't we want to get the bureaucrats out of the lives of our members?

The issue of how we are to govern and fund our schools is much more complicated than whether the money should merely be passed back to the states or kept in Washington. First, we must state that, generally speaking, those closest to the solution should have more say in solving the problem. That is why conceptually AASA has supported the notion of reducing regulation and moving authority back to local districts. However, this is a far cry from the new federalism that is being proposed in Washington these days. What is being proposed is moving power back to the states. Even a cursory examination shows that state capitals are reluctant to return power or resources to local school districts. Most states have either reduced or severely curtailed education spending. Many states have enacted legislation that directly diminishes the powers, prestige and in some cases remuneration of local school leaders. Returning power to the governors without guarantees that a similar return to local control is forthcoming is not in education's best interest.

Frankly, many states have an abysmal record of dealing with equity issues or with protecting children. There are tremendous inequities within states in spending for education (as well as tremendous inequities between states). The inequities between states will not be cured or helped by block granting funds to states and there is no guarantee that such money will be used within states to deal with equity issues.

In terms of protecting children, the record is just as sad. More than 40 percent of children who have died from abuse or neglect were known to state agencies before they died; still, they were not protected. Nearly two dozen states are currently under court order because of their dismal record in protecting children. States tend to put their resources at the wrong end of the pipeline. Instead of investing in children, they invest in prisons.

The idea of block grants is appealing but their record makes them suspect. The history of block grants is to block and cut. The good news is states get more flexibility. The bad news is states have less federal money to spend. Further, the history of block grants to states is that they pass on the financial burden to the locals. As the support for the hungry and homeless is reduced, they will be lining up at the local agencies for help. And these agencies will have fewer resources to meet the challenge. This snowball rolling down the hill ultimately will crash against the schoolhouse door.

You will be forced to pick up the cost of serving an even greater proportion of your children who are hungry, sick or abused.

Why the big fuss over the federal education dollar, since it is only about 6 percent of the average school budget? In part because the average is deceiving. First, federal money has been used by most districts to fill voids created by inadequate state and local support. Does anyone seriously believe that as federal dollars disappear, state and local support for technology and staff development will increase? Anyway, that 6 percent is illusory. For many districts it amounts to 1 or 2 percent. These tend to be the districts that wonder why we are fighting for these dollars, since they hardly seem worth it. When I was superintendent in Princeton, for example, we got virtually no federal money. The money we did get helped serve the few at-risk students in the district, and we had some small grants to do staff development and curriculum work. A loss of federal dollars would have pained, for a while, but would not have lowered our SAT scores.

However, for other districts, the federal dollars represent 10 to 15 percent of their budgets. These tend to be districts with higher percentages of children in poverty. For them, the reductions are devastating. When I was superintendent in Tucson, Ariz., the federal dollars were critical to serving a vast and growing number of students who came to school with serious gaps and tremendous social and economic handicaps. The percentage of our budget from federal money was well over 10 percent and a cut in revenue would have badly damaged the district's ability to cope with tremendous challenges. Federal money has been used, to a great extent, to try to address inequity of opportunity to learn.

As for the federal "bureaucrats," well, a "bureaucrat" exists in the eye of the beholder. I always thought a bureaucrat was anyone who stood between me and what I wanted. What one person calls a bureaucrat, another calls a "superintendent," "assistant superintendent," or a "director" or even a "principal." We should be cautious of falling into the name-calling routine, for the name you call someone else may well get pinned on you.

Yes, we agree with you, that as local leaders, you should have more opportunity to chart your own path to the future. But we want to make certain that you have adequate provisions and protection from the dangers you will encounter. And we want to make sure that if you are attacked you get lots of support. Most of all, as child advocates, we want to make certain that those with the greatest need are not left behind.

᠁

In 1996, we celebrated the 200th anniversary of the birthday of Horace Mann, the father of American public schools. The Horace Mann League commemorated the event, in part, by surveying educators about the top 10 biggest threats to U.S. public schools. The results said much about the perils facing us in today's world.

☙

On Schools' 200th Anniversary, Threats Loom Large

T his past year I had the honor of serving as president of the Horace Mann League. The Horace Mann League is an organization dedicated to upholding the beliefs and ideals of Horace Mann, the father of the public school movement in America. May 4, 1996, marks the 200th anniversary of the birth of Horace Mann, and consequently, the birth of public schools in this country.

Horace Mann believed that America needed a system of common schools to perpetuate the ideals of our democracy and to provide a unifying vision for American life. The league, like Horace Mann himself, believes our public schools should be free and without discrimination based on class, religious beliefs, race or nationality.

Tragically, in this anniversary year, we are facing the very real possibility that Mann's dream is merely a fading memory. I say this based on a poll the league conducted of its members, the results of which were released at its annual meeting during the National Conference on Education©.

The survey of leading educators reveals what they feel are the top 10 most destructive factors influencing public education. They are:

✤ At No. 10, a tie between **public resistance to change**, based on often outdated notions of schooling, and **labor unions' resistance to change**, in the form of collective bargaining agreements. People want better schools, but not different ones. Yet if we continue to do what we've always done, we'll continue to get what we've always gotten. I have spent a lot of time and effort defending our schools from unwarranted criticism because I think we are scapegoats much of the time. However, we must change schools dramatically; I say this because, while we have been improving over time, we are doing a better and better job at the wrong thing. The mission of educating all children to high standards, rather than creaming the best students, is a new mission. It will require dramatic effort and change.

✤ The ninth most destructive threat, according to the survey, is the constant drumbeat from **voucher proponents** to end public education as we know it and, in particular, to drive public funding to schools that may be segregated by religion, race or socioeconomic level.

✤ The eighth most destructive factor — all too familiar to educators who have witnessed school communities torn apart by competing political interests — is **the influence of the religious right** on federal, state and local statutes and policies. Just how popular schools have become as a platform for pushing through a narrow agenda is evident in the comment by Ralph Reed, executive director of the Christian Coalition, that he would rather elect 2,000 school board members than a U.S. president.

The seventh most destructive factor is **the inattention to social issues**. Among these are poverty; lack of health care; children unprepared to enter school; and racial, religious and linguistic diversity that is not properly supported. In the words of the late Ernest Boyer, "We cannot have islands of academic excellence in a sea of community indifference."

The sixth most destructive influence are **school board members who pander to the electorate**, lack political astuteness, micromanage districts or reflect the narrow agendas of special interests. This is not a broad indictment of local governance, it is a call for responsible leadership.

The fifth most destructive factor is **the inability of educators to see different schools for the future**. For Horace Mann's dream to live, and for common schools to survive, superintendents must provide leadership to transform our institutions. Schools in the 21st century cannot look like the ones Mann developed in the 19th.

Compounding the problem, at No. 4, are **citizens lacking a sense of responsibility for the entire community's public schools**. This is evidenced by special initiatives for one's own school and aggravated by the transient nature of community residents in this highly mobile society.

The third most dangerous factor is **the way we currently fund public schools**. This includes over-reliance on property taxes, inequitable distribution of funds and mandates from the states and federal government that come without money attached.

The second greatest threat is **the decline of the family**. Dramatic shifts in family structure and ever-greater pressures on both two- and one-parent households mean schools are being asked to deliver an ever-broader array of services, including before- and after-school care, health services, meals, and multilingual instruction, as well as a stellar academic program.

&. The No. 1 threat to public education is something I have spent much of my time and energy fighting, and that is **the perpetuated negative myths about public education**. This is something each of us must work on overcoming and something organizations such as the Horace Mann League and AASA must continue to put at the top of our agendas. It is clear from the other "threats" that public schools have many problems to overcome. But when the greatest problem is spurious, we really have to worry.

I personally believe that some would like to end common schools as created by Horace Mann, and they are using false information to worsen the public's confidence in our system of public schools. I believe that if we let that happen, the American values envisioned by our founding fathers, which have been the basis of the dream that has driven this country for more than 200 hundred years, will come to a sad and tragic end.

Clearly, the way to contend with the dangerous factors facing public education will be through thoughtful, forceful and courageous leadership by those of us who are responsible for keeping the dream alive and the common school a place for building America the Beautiful.

It is amazing what happens when you advocate for children. While the job is good for your soul, it can sometimes be confusing. In spring 1996, AASA received attention from both ends of the political spectrum. On the one hand, we supported the Stand for Children, a march on Washington to dramatize the needs of our most vulnerable citizens — our children — and were praised by child advocates. On the other, we published a study that pointed out that schools have a responsibility to teach virtue in various forms, which got us praise from the Christian Coalition. Our thinking was simply this: You must do right by kids and expect kids to do what's right as well. It's not rocket science.

༈

We Must Reach Agreement on Behalf of Children

A t the National Conference on Education© this year, we began the First General Session with Marian Wright Edelman of the Children's Defense Fund, who is probably the strongest advocate for children in America today. We concluded the conference with Jonathan Kozol, who is, perhaps, the most eloquent writer on behalf of children today. That combination was not accidental. It arose from my conviction that our jobs must begin and end with children: Children must be the Alpha and Omega of school leaders. To the extent we forget that, we fail in our responsibilities.

AASA recently has received some interesting attention because we are taking a stand for children; that attention has come from both ends of the political spectrum. We have scored points on the "liberal" side for supporting children's funding, welfare reform that protects children, advocating an investment trust fund, and enthusiastically supporting the Stand for Children march, which will be held on June 1. On the other hand, we recently were featured on Christian radio and praised by the Christian Coalition for the work we did on the "Preparing Children for the 21st Century" report, which called for building greater responsibility and for promoting ethics and values.

While widely disparate groups have reacted positively to different parts of our agenda, the fact is, we have been consistent in our message. We are leveling an area of common ground that may help heal some of the violent disagreements currently rending our country.

It is simply a matter of understanding that there are actions that we must take for children and there are actions that must be done by children for themselves. We cannot expect little babies to feed themselves, to clothe themselves, to minister to their illnesses, or to protect themselves. We adults must take responsibility for them. Now that opinion seems to have become a "liberal" position. That is why people like Marian Wright Edelman and Jonathan Kozol have been branded liberals. They are fearless and indefatigable in calling for better support and more resources for children.

Conversely, we also must see that children learn to be responsible for their own behavior, that they treat each other with kindness and respect, and that they learn the value of hard work and ingenuity. That has been a view claimed by the "conservatives." The fact is, raising children, nurturing children, and loving children is not a liberal or a conservative position — it's a human position and we must all do better at it than we have.

Doing the right thing for children seems to be an economic issue. After all, it costs money to take care of poor children. It might even mean income redistribution. That is viewed as a "Robin Hood" approach. Giving children job skills to ready them for the marketplace is an economic imperative. It assumes that the reason we educate is to create income potential for the child and economic possibilities for society. However, I am reminded of the idea proffered by Albert Einstein — that no problem is ever solved at the level at which it was created.

Poverty and its implications clearly are economic in origin and nature, but their solutions are ultimately not economic. The solution to poverty in this country ultimately must be a moral one. The moral plane is a higher plane than the economic. One will never be able to mount sufficient economic reasons to make those who have resources surrender them to benefit those who do not. If you try to build a cost-benefit ratio argument, or a prevention argument, it will only go so far and you will get a lot of "yes, buts" in response. Humans can always find reasons to be selfish. As one writer has suggested, humans are not rational animals nearly so much as we are rationalizing animals. However, on the moral plane there are no excuses or rationalizations.

Kozol told his audience at the AASA conference that the bottom line of his book was a quote from Jesus, who said, "If you love me, feed my sheep." That doesn't leave a lot of room for "yes, buts." When one notes that we must "suffer the little children — for theirs is the kingdom of God," there is little room for discussions of policy or taxes, flat or rounded. When it is suggested that "in as much as you have done it unto the least of these, you have done it unto me," there is no need for research or new policy.

The fact is that children form a common ground for us in this country whether you are a member of the "religious" right or the "irreligious" left. As a nation, we are restricting our future by our failure to protect children and by our failure to expect the best from them.

The Stand for Children march on June 1 is a tangible statement that we are prepared to support and love all children the way we love our own. I hope many of you will find a way to join us here in Washington with your families and members of your communities. I know that for those who live a great distance from Washington, this will be difficult. But you might be surprised by the response if you invite people. Further, I would hope each community across the country would plan a Stand for Children activity on the Sunday following the demonstration, as organizers are urging, so that the nation will be focused on the needs of children and how they can be met in every community across the country. This is a chance to reinvigorate our national dialogue, policy direction and personal commitment with regard to children.

Yes, we must help our children pull themselves up by their own bootstraps by being responsible and taking charge of their values and actions. But we must also see that they have boots to wear, and that is an adult responsibility.

ॐ

More reading ideas. This time the focus is on leadership but from very different places. Two of the books are from highly successful NBA coaches with different styles and philosophies. One focuses on building teams as the job of any good leader; the other ties the spiritual side of leadership into the mix. The third book is in praise of paradox, the most frustrating and empowering aspect of modern leadership.

&

Teamwork, Spirit, and the Absurd: 3 Summer Reads

As a school leader I always looked forward to summer as a time to renew and recharge my batteries. Much of this renewal came from having some time to catch up on my reading. Now that much of my job involves traveling from place to place to meet with you and speak to groups of educators and others, I have frequent uninterrupted reading time on long airplane flights. So, I'd like to offer some suggestions for your summer reading.

The first two books, *The Winner Within: A Life Plan for Team Players* by Pat Riley and *Sacred Hoops: Spiritual Lessons of a Hardwood Warrior* by Phil Jackson, come from the world of professional basketball. I know school leaders are often faulted as ex-coaches who were put in charge of schools once they lost their winning touch. However, because I never coached, I read Riley's book objectively and found that coaching in the NBA and running schools have more in common than we might like to admit.

First, neither the coach nor the school leader has any authority because of title. Each is responsible without really being in charge. If the team loses, the coach is dismissed, not the team. And one has to balance a variety of massive egos, each wanting to go his own way and play his own game.

It was my interest in management, however, that drew me to Riley's book. He is best known for coaching the L.A. Lakers during the 1980s, when they won several championships.

Riley's basic premise is that teamwork is the essence of life. If done properly, teamwork blends the individual talents and strengths of team members into a "force that becomes greater than the sum of the parts." Riley believes that "great teamwork is the only way to reach ultimate moments that create the breakthroughs that define our careers and fulfill our lives with a sense of lasting significance."

Building a team is not simple. Riley says that you must begin with a sense of "innocence," trusting in the team. Far too often we see teamwork erode through mistrust and freelancing on the part of individuals. Psychologist Wayne Dyer calls that "cancerous" action, when one cell decides to do its own thing at the expense of the other cells. Ultimately, it destroys itself as well as others.

Riley points out that innocence is different from naiveté. Being naïve is failing to understand threats to your territory. Innocence acknowledges the threat and sets it aside for the greater good. Closely connected to a sense of innocence is overcoming the "disease of me." The "disease of me" is evidenced by an overwhelming sense of self-importance. Riley not only describes the disease but prescribes the cure — a covenant that binds people together and builds a foundation for mutual support.

The Winner Within is filled with useful insights, and is sprinkled with inspirational quotes. Riley relates real-life examples to make his points, which makes it a good book for ex-coaches, but an excellent book for anyone trying to build teamwork.

The other book, by Phil Jackson, coach of the Chicago Bulls and the most winning coach of the 1990s, reveals that Jackson relies on a sense of "spirituality." Like Riley, Jackson has been blessed by great players, but players with large egos. Yet he too has been able to blend their talents into an awesome team.

Jackson shares the spiritual lessons he learned first growing up as a minister's child, and then later in his quest for answers that led him to explore Eastern religions and the beliefs of Native Americans. He has managed to blend these diverse spiritual views together just as deftly as he has been able to blend the talents of Michael Jordan, Scottie Pippen and Dennis Rodman.

The centerpiece of Jackson's world view is a sense of "mindfulness." "Mindfulness" stresses awareness, compassion and selfless team play. Jackson takes the lessons of Zen and Native American warriors to create a sense of acting with a clear mind, respecting the enemy, and being aggressive without anger. He stresses the need to live in the moment and to stay calmly focused amid chaos, so that "the 'me' becomes the servant of 'we.'"

Jackson feels that the way to forge winners is to call on the players' need to connect with something larger than themselves. The trick to staying focused on this is to experience each moment with a clear mind and an open heart. Jackson reminds us that the wise leader is a leader of service, that he or she is receptive and that the real art of leadership is learning to follow.

Among the many lessons Jackson offers is one from Albert Einstein who; taught that "out of clutter, find simplicity; from discord, find harmony; and in the middle of difficulty lies opportunity."

This leads to my final book suggestion — a very unconventional look at leadership by Richard Farson called *Management of the Absurd: Paradoxes in Leadership*. Farson has a unique and powerful way of looking at the challenges of leadership by pointing out that leadership in today's world is embracing paradox. Farson organizes his book around 33 paradoxes. Some quotes from Farson:

- "The opposite of a profound truth is also a profound truth."
- "Once you find a management technique that works, give it up."
- "Technology creates the opposite of the intended purpose."
- "Listening is more difficult than talking."

Farson ends his book of management advice with a chapter titled, "My advice is, don't take my advice." His point is that we should reflect on what we ought to do, not blindly follow what others tell us. This is also part of what Jackson means by being mindful and what Riley means by the innocence of setting aside what we know for a greater purpose.

Whether you choose to read these books, or others, or merely to sit and think about what you're doing, I hope you will use the pause in your harried schedule to refresh and renew yourself for the coming challenges. We all have a cause greater than ourselves to carry forward and it deserves our best effort. And, to do that, we have to occasionally take care of ourselves.

Sometimes what you label a thing or a person becomes limiting. For years, we have been content to label some of our children "at risk," so they have been. The Stand for Children march, which brought hundreds of thousands of child advocates to Washington, offered us the opportunity to do something about those who are labelled "at risk." It also challenged us to see our children differently.

৽৹

How Does America Define Its Children? 'At-Risk' Label Can Limit Their Promise

Recently, I had a vivid reminder of why I chose education as a profession, when I attended two very different meetings in two different cities.

The first was the Stand for Children march in Washington on June 1. AASA was one of more than 3,000 different groups that supported the rally. It was a spectacular day in Washington for several reasons. First, spring has been late this year and the rally coincided with one of our loveliest days so far. Second, more than 200,000 people converged on the Lincoln Memorial grounds to remind all of us that, as a nation, we can do better for our children. Parents, grandparents, teachers, administrators, child advocates and others came together for a few short hours to embrace this belief.

AASA was represented by our Executive Committee, our staff and numerous members from all over the country. Many of us staked out a spot in the sun where we had a good view of the stage. We were illuminated by both efforts. The first major portion of the program was devoted to children's singing and to a number of prayers offered by representatives of the major religions of the world.

The speeches were by ordinary citizens with extraordinary insight. One young lady from Southern California announced that she was a 15-year-old Latina who lived in a neighborhood impacted by poverty and crime. She could not understand how children could go hungry or how teenagers could kill each other because of frivolous causes, and she hoped she would never be old enough to understand that.

Another speaker was a father whose son was murdered by a 14-year-old boy. In his grief he realized that on that evening America had lost two children, and they were both victims of the gun. It was a compelling and moving story, as were all the stories shared that afternoon.

Two of the speakers were familiar to AASA conference attendees: Geoffrey Canada, who was passionate and eloquent on the issues facing children in this country, and the leader of the Stand for Children march, Marian Wright Edelman, who put the rally into the moral context in which it belonged.

Just prior to the march, representatives of the Christian Coalition and the Heritage Foundation spoke acidly of the rally as another attempt to build up the welfare state, but the substance of the rally showed how hollow the thinking of these critics was. The emphasis of the Stand was not on government, although it was pointed out that government certainly bears a role in correcting the ills of our society. As Marian Wright Edelman stated, we are not seeking a big government, but a just one. Priorities should be placed on children before capital gains tax reductions or extra weapon systems that the Pentagon does not want.

The greater emphasis that day, though, was on people taking greater personal responsibility for children, building strong families and strong communities. As Edelman said, "This is a day about rekindling our children's hopes and renewing our faith in each other and in our great nation's future." The rhetoric of the rally was positive. No blame was levied. As columnist Molly Ivins pointed out, "No one dissed Newt Gingrich or cussed the Republicans or Congress or the President. The speakers just asked them and us to do better."

More persuasive than the rhetoric was the picture the march presented. It was America at its best. We talk a lot about being a melting pot and about our diversity, but we rarely see it in such vividness. As columnist Bob Herbert stated in *The New York Times*, "The odds on the nation's future would look pretty good to anyone who took the time to stroll the acreage between the Washington Monument and the Lincoln Memorial—It was a study in inclusiveness, the most thoroughly and comfortably integrated large crowd I have ever seen. It was a crowd that spoke—in its commitment, its decency and its variety—to the real possibilities of America. It was the way America might look if its promise were ever realized."

I was proud to lend my voice to the effort and to see America's school leaders standing for children.

Meanwhile, the other meeting I attended took place in Boston. It was called by U.S. Secretary of Education Richard Riley and Attorney General Janet Reno to look at the issue of youth who are not in the mainstream. I joined other educators, police chiefs, prosecuting attorneys, youth leaders and others who came together to look at troubled youths—those who are having a difficult time making the transition to productive adulthood. We are currently having a number of debates on "zero tolerance" and "cessation of services" and what have you. The question that I pondered at the conference was how far out can we kick kids? We can expel them from school, but we can't expel them from society.

The highlight of the meeting for me was an inspiring talk by Mervlyn Kitashima, who is a native Hawaiian and works for the state Department of Education in Hawaii. Mervlyn now holds a very responsible position, although she was once a student "at risk." In fact, she suggested we start by no longer using that term. When we label someone, we limit them. If we insist on labels, she suggested we start using the term "at promise" because that is what we are really hoping to see. Children and youth are at promise of making a good life for themselves and contributing to society. Mervlyn discovered that, as an adult, she was part of an extensive long-term study being done on "at-risk" ("at-promise!") children, and that much had been learned from the study about why some students succeed and some do not. Mervlyn shared her insights with us. She suggested that children need to learn the value of work. It is rewarding and it establishes good habits such as effort and responsibility. She was also given small acts of kindness by others. She was showered with caring and affirmation. She was offered education as an option in order to create a future for herself.

She suggested that we, as adults, need to do two more things. First, we must take risks for kids. It is easy to cut them off. It is much more difficult to believe in them. She also suggested that we give kids hope—we must help them believe that something better is in store for them. There are no bad kids, but kids who have bad problems. The first step is helping them believe in something beyond themselves. This is really what the Stand for Children was about and really what our jobs are day to day. If we can put more faith in our children and give them a sense of faith in themselves, we can make many more days bright with the sunshine of their hope.

❧

One of the greatest problems critics of public education have is telling the truth. Many seem to believe that distorting the record to show everyone how bad schools are is the best way to get school people to improve. I have called this the attempt to bludgeon people to greatness. The truth is that schools have done a remarkably good job working in difficult circumstances, and there is much more that can and should be done. It is quite rare to find a national study that understands and articulates this balance and offers good ideas for improving the things that need improvement. The Consortium on Productivity (underwritten by the Ball Foundation) managed to offer such a report, and it is still well worth studying.

જ⁊

Design Flaws in American System Make It Hard To Improve

I t is a rare occasion when we find a national report on education that is positive and makes sense. Imagine my excitement at running across such a document. The Consortium on Productivity in the Schools has produced a report called "Using What We Have To Get the Schools We Need: A Productivity Focus for American Education." Don't let the title put you off. The report is worth study.

It is useful for its conclusions about the current status of American education. Contrary to popular opinion and blasts from the critics and the media, the report makes several key and startling points. First, since the mid-1970s, student performance as measured by test scores has not declined, but has remained stable. What this means is that a consortium of serious academicians and hard-headed businesspeople has reached the same conclusions found by the Sandia researchers and other "contrarians" such as Gerald Bracey and David Berliner.

The consortium also found that real per-pupil spending for K-12 education has increased, but not by as much as most people think. The increase has been greatly influenced by rising costs for special education. Again, in total alignment with Sandia, Bracey and the lesser known but powerful work of Richard Rothstein. Finally, the report notes that over time the environment in which schools are teaching and students are learning has become less conducive to learning. This acknowledges that context influences how well kids do—a concept understood by most educators and ignored by many lawmakers and policymakers.

In fact, the report states that "productivity in education has held steady over the past 20 years, not declined. In fact—based on current demographics, increased poverty of the school population, and current resources, we might have predicted school and student performance that is worse than it is now."

So what's the problem? We seem to be doing well under difficult circumstances. Quite simply, what we're doing will not be enough to ensure that our students and our country can succeed in today's difficult environment. We need to find ways to be even more effective under increasingly difficult circumstances—a task most educational leaders know is at the core of their mission. Thankfully, the report offers help with that task.

First, the authors surveyed other fields to see what can be learned. What they found is startling: American children do not attend school for significantly less time than children from other countries. Our year is shorter, but our days are longer. However, we are not getting the most from the time we spend on education, because of design flaws such as the artificial breakup of time into periods. Also, we try to teach too many things to kids, leading us to stray from a central focus. We also make very limited use of non-school time with homework.

Other findings of note:

America spends very little on educational research and development compared with other industries. Federal research on energy accounts for 55 percent of the total expenditures; for space science, it is 50 percent. In defense it is 13 percent. And in education—a mere 0.8 percent.

The report looks at the entire system. The authors break down the system into eight subsystems: governance, management, financing, teaching and learning, adaptive and innovative, hiring and purchasing, outplacement, and maintenance. They then analyze each of the subsystems to see how well they function.

Unfortunately, none of them are functioning close to capacity. And according to the authors, it begins with a breakdown at the governance level. Governance sets goals and quality standards, resolves conflicts among constituents and among those doing the governing, and raises and allocates resources. It begins with goals, and tragically, ends there for the American system. Effective goals are limited in number, are stable and unchanging, are focused on the first mission of the sector, are focused on outcomes, are translated into clear performance standards, and are understood and accepted as legitimate.

The authors, when viewing these measures against the current governance system of American schools found that goals are unstable and multiply. This fuels a negative spiral that creates declining customer expectations (goal erosion) and thus endangers the political and financial support needed for the system to survive. The political nature of the system lies at the heart of the problem. The report states that "the United States has less an education system than a political system that purports to provide education."

Because goals are unstable and proliferating, it is virtually impossible for management to align resources to the goals and the spiral spins downward still. Teaching and learning is structured to reinforce continuity, not continuous improvement. Unstable goals encourage teachers to ignore external demands and the web of top-down regulations marginalizes the effects of variations in management within the school. And so it goes throughout each of the subsystems.

The clear analysis of the problems created by a breakdown in the system would be contribution enough to the profession, but the authors go further by providing some ideas for improvement. These include pointing out ways the contract between governance and management should be renegotiated by trading autonomy for accountability. The report also strongly suggests that funding formulas be linked to clarifying where the money is spent, and to increased standards of productivity. And there is more.

Bottom line? We're better than we're given credit for being, doing good work under difficult circumstances; but we're not nearly as good as we need to be to face the new realities of our society and our mission. And we're worse at that than most of us imagine. But we can do it better. Getting better will mean that we must look at the entire system and fix it by increasing its capacity to improve productivity.

The good news is that there is a clear need for system leaders and someone out there understands the perils to your effectiveness and the promise of your leadership.

Watching the effects of the electoral process in Washington is like watching the sap rise in the trees. Or should I say "saps"? It makes for some silly happenings. During a few pre-election months, Congress went from taking actions with potentially long-term negative effects on children to, in an almost complete turnaround on school funding, appropriating money for education just before members had to go back home and explain themselves. I thought it might be nice to focus on key questions we might ask those who would represent us . . .

ॐ

Welcome to Another School Year— Another Election Season

One of the treasures of our business in education is that, unlike most other enterprises, we get a fresh start every year. This is the time of the year when children's hearts beat a little faster and school administrators' palms sweat a bit more as we contemplate the coming year with its opportunities and risks. Like all those before it, this year will be a rollercoaster ride.

Living in Washington, I am a bit jaded by the atmosphere here, and I have been thinking about what the year might bring politically. We continue to have excellent leadership and representation by our Secretary of Education Richard Riley. It matters not what your political affiliation might be, if you are an educator, you have to appreciate his clear, calm, consistent voice of reason and decency. In a city where such things are often in short supply, he towers. That is not to say we always agree with the department's positions. In fact, we have significant objections to some of the current administration's approaches to key issues. It is much easier, nonetheless, to disagree agreeably when you can respect the point-person. Not all of our secretaries of education met this expectation.

BACK-TO-SCHOOL

Secretary Riley has asked all the major education organizations to use back-to-school season to help the nation refocus on its schools and its children. The initiative is called "America Goes Back to School." AASA President Don Thompson serves on the national steering committee for this worthwhile campaign. The thrust is to encourage schools to connect to their communities by having various events that will engage adults— parents or not—in their local schools.

Such efforts might include student- or principal-for-a-day programs to enlighten adults about education today. Also, community members might be invited to speak to students about their work or a civic issue. The content is much less important than the process — adults and kids engaging each other, and by doing so, reaffirming the place of schools in the life of the community. While the initiative kicked off this month, it is viewed as a year-long effort, and we hope every school leader in America will find ways to involve their communities. For more information, call (800) USA LEARN.

SUMMER TO REMEMBER

Meanwhile, back on the Hill, the politics continue. August saw a flurry of activity from Congress and President Bill Clinton, both trying to prove to the American public that they are doing a good job. Many of the bills passed will have profound effect on your work. Most troubling was the so-called "Welfare Reform Act"—a bill to end welfare as we've come to know it, to paraphrase the president. Essentially it moves the responsibility and decision making for this program back to the states.

While everyone agrees changes are necessary, I believe that the long-term impact will be a serious reduction in benefits to children. More children likely will come to your doors even less well cared for than they are now. Further, the pressure of competition for limited state dollars will, in most cases, not accrue to the benefit of schools. As more destitution invades society, dollars that might otherwise have gone to education will have to be funneled to other areas. Educators are going to get squeezed from both ends, with more problems and fewer resources.

One glaring problem with this bill, which is full of problems, involves denying all welfare benefits to any parent who has been convicted of a drug-related offense. This means that the children of such parents also would be denied benefits. It's a classic case of the sins of the parent being visited upon the children. Further, this parent does not need to be the custodial parent. Anyone who has fathered a child in or out of wedlock, in or out of the home, could cause the child to lose AFDC support. Incredible! AASA, along with other child advocates, fought the good fight and lost. We lost it because, ironically enough, for the first time in years, this issue became nonpartisan—the president was as eager to get a bill passed as Congress was. We believe it was a bad choice for both Congress and the president.

The issue of immigration also continues to be emotional and difficult. From an educators' perspective, we probably will see schools squeezed as benefits for immigrants are reduced or cut, but with needy people still among us. And, if those who wish to deny immigrants an education succeed, which seems a possibility, no one has yet suggested what we, as a society, do with those who go uneducated. Once again, we see political expediency usurp the needs of children.

FOR OR AGAINST CHILDREN?

With the presidential campaign in full swing, we will see more duck-billed platitudes designed to appeal to our worst fears and prejudices. At present, funding for education next year looks shaky, despite both parties' vows to be for education. Already, vouchers are the cornerstone of one party's education platform. Still, we cannot be partisan in our approach. In fact, we feel strongly that the future of education lies in the political center. We need the support of moderates from both parties. This was my rule of thumb at the local level, where it never made any difference whether I was getting beaten on the right side of the head or the left side; the pain was just as real. The responsible middle is where we have to find our help. Neither political party has a corner on virtue or viciousness, and we should not delude ourselves into thinking otherwise.

QUESTIONS TO ASK

With that in mind, I ask that you ask the following questions to determine whether a particular candidate would be a worthy officeholder from the perspective of our children and their future:

1. How will you demonstrate your commitment to children—all children—in your policies? (There are a lot of people in America who have no commitment to children, other than their own and those of their friends.)

2. Do you consider children an investment or a cost, and which policies that you espouse demonstrate your perspective? (The philosophy underlying many programs today is that children are a cost to be contained and not an investment we make for our future and society as a whole.)

3. Are schools an economic entity or a public good, and what actions would you take to show your bias on this question? (Schools began as a public good, but now are viewed by many merely as a source of workers and a strong economy. Policies that revolve around vouchers and competition are a by-product of such thinking. Competition accepts losers as natural law. In our case these losers are someone's children.)

4. What, if anything, would you do about the great disparities that exist among schools-communities in their ability to serve children? (Educators often are judged as a unified system by politicians, who fail to deal with the reasons we have good schools and poor schools. Students from homes with higher incomes do better in school than those who live in poverty. Communities that spend more on schools get higher achievement and more children going to college. Those graduates make more money when they get out of school. Per-pupil spending does have a significant impact on education and after-school earnings.)

5. Do you feel that school professionals or changing social dynamics of our country are to blame for educational problems? (Most politicians in this country just don't get it. They ignore progress that has been made, and fail to offer realistic solutions for the complex issues that confront us.)

So, here we go again. As one of the freshmen congressmen used to sing, "the beat goes on." Another year. Another quadrennial election. Another challenge and opportunity for us to stand and be counted for the children and schools.

We've all heard that good things come in small packages. And when it comes to school size and district size, the research definitely shows it to be true. Therefore, I think it's time for us to begin to reverse the long-term trend of making our schools bigger.

≈

Thinking Small Makes a Big Difference

As we all know, education reform comes in many guises. One of the challenges for school people involves selecting the right plan and finding the "leverage" points to move a new idea into practice. I would like to make a modest, yet somewhat radical proposal to make schools and school districts smaller in the future or to find ways to "demassify" what we are already doing.

Education has wandered for at least 40 years in the wilderness of "bigger is better." This came from James Bryant Conant's landmark study on comprehensive high schools and from our American penchant for efficiency. Actually, school district consolidation started long before Conant took pen to paper. Since the end of World War II, we have decreased the number of school districts by 70 percent. We still find states pressing to reduce the number of districts through consolidation. Meanwhile, our population keeps growing. The average school population today is 5 times what it was 50 years ago.

Perhaps in earlier days consolidation made sense. The world was a simpler place then. But with the deterioration of our social structure, schools are being called upon to step in and play a much broader role in the lives of children. But they're being asked to do so in an increasingly impersonal environment. In this context, big doesn't work, but small can.

A recent study from the Northwest Regional Laboratory in Portland, Ore., shows that small schools are superior to large ones on almost every measure. Kathleen Cotton, author of the report, looked at more than 100 research studies concerning the relationship between school size and different aspects of schooling. When small schools are not superior to large ones, they're just as good. This is true for both elementary and secondary schools, and it is true for students of all ability groups and in every town and city in this country.

While the term "small" can have many interpretations, for the sake of this discussion, I refer to schools of roughly 400 to 500 students.

Conant believed that larger schools offered a greater variety in curriculum. Yet Cotton found that a 100 percent increase in enrollment generated only a 17 percent increase in courses offered. What normally happens in larger schools is that the richer curriculum is made up, not necessarily of higher level courses, but of additional introductory courses in non-core areas. Researchers found that only 5 to 12 percent of the students in larger schools even avail themselves of the extra courses these schools typically offer.

In other words, a 400-student school generally can offer a curriculum that compares quite favorably in terms of breadth and depth with curricula offered in much larger schools. With the emphasis on core learning as a common standard, in fact, many large schools are winnowing down their curricula anyway. And with distance learning and other technologies, the curriculum can be expanded in small schools without consolidation.

Of course, every state legislator and businessperson will tell you that you need larger schools because they allow "economies of scale." However, Cotton found that the research does not support this either. If small high schools do not try to duplicate the infrastructure of large schools, they can be very economical. One of the reasons such a large portion of the per-pupil expenditures in America does not touch the classroom is not because of too many administrators, as some would say, but because there is too much of everything. Large size requires more monitoring and more record-keeping, which requires more people and greater expenditures. Smallness simplifies discipline and counseling.

What about academic achievement? Cotton's review indicates that about half the studies find no difference in achievement and none found large schools superior. No matter how you look at it, student achievement in small schools is at least equal, and often superior, to student achievement in large schools. This includes such things as grades, test scores, honor roll, subject area achievement and higher-order thinking skills. Size of graduating class makes no difference in college GPA or the likelihood of graduating with a degree.

Further, student attitudes in small schools are more positive. Students in small schools have higher attendance rates, are less likely to drop out, and express a much greater sense of belonging than do their counterparts in larger schools. Small schools have fewer incidents of negative social behavior. Part of the explanation for this is that students who engage in extracurricular activities tend to behave better and student participation in such activities is significantly higher in small schools than in large ones. These benefits are not limited to small rural schools. They cut across settings.

Certainly larger schools can, and do, offer more varied activities than small ones, but the average student in a large school does not take advantage of these opportunities.

Why does smallness work? The research reveals several answers. First, everything is just easier. Smallness requires participation, which creates engagement. It's hard to get lost in a small school. And it's hard to hide. People come to know each other and to care for each other. Both parents and students are more involved. Teachers in small schools are more likely to form teaching teams, integrate their subject matter, and employ multi-age grouping and cooperative learning. In addition, small schools have a greater emphasis on experiential learning that is relevant to the outside world.

Of particular note is that students living in poverty, and racial and ethnic minorities—who currently are concentrated largely in urban areas with big schools—benefit from smaller schools.

Despite all these findings, it will be difficult to overcome the decades of belief that bigger is better and change attitudes to support smallness. As a practical matter, we are stuck with generations of schools that were built with "big" in mind. However, a part of leadership is finding and promoting workable alternatives. A starting point is to discuss the facts, and not add further to the problem by promoting largeness in the decisions we make. We can take advantage of the benefits of smallness by creating schools-within-schools, for example. The first step, though, is to understand that thinking big sometimes starts by thinking small.

ze

What we need in school leadership today is more of the C word — courage. And the strongest dose of courage is required for us to take a long look at ourselves and ask who we are and what are we about.

આ

Leadership Takes
Courage and Conviction

L eadership requires self-knowledge. Two key questions for the leader are "Who am I?" and "Why am I here?" These also are the critical questions for a leadership organization. In the turbulent and contentious world of today's schools, a major reason for our existence as individual leaders, or as an organization such as AASA, or as state organizations of school administrators, is to display courage.

If acting courageously is not what we are about, then we are taking up valuable space and, through our inaction, adding to educational problems. I hope you see your national organization as one that will take risks on behalf of school leaders and the children we serve. I am also heartened when I see examples of courage expressed by our members and state affiliates. As the saying goes, "You have to go out on a limb to pick the sweetest fruit."

A different sort of courage is required to listen to those with whom we may disagree, but it is the civil thing to do and we may learn something. Recently, I have heard concerns about AASA inviting former vice-president Dan Quayle to speak at our national conference. As a member of the Bush administration, he had some rather tough sledding with the press and his critics for his conservative views, if not for his spelling. Last year we had a few people who didn't like Marian Wright Edelman and Jonathan Kozol because they were perceived as being too liberal.

The fact is, we are a large national organization made up of members from across the political spectrum, and we have an obligation to present many views, knowing that some people will not always like what we offer. Speaking out on your behalf, I ask for your forgiveness if I occasionally say something that does not fit your personal views. The reality is, we can't press for all the issues we have to worry about without going out on a limb occasionally, and we can't provide a balanced national conference without providing a variety of viewpoints, even those with whom we disagree.

Personally, I disagree with many of Quayle's ideas, particularly about education, but I am looking forward to hearing his views on family and parent involvement, which he outlines in his new book, *The American Family: Discovering the Values that Make Us Strong*, and which is the theme of this year's conference. Like it or not, he put "family values" on the political screen, and in the four years since he took on Murphy Brown, family values have dominated much of the political discussion, and will continue to do so for some time to come.

If you don't want to hear Quayle, you can spend some family time at Disney World; or come listen to Lester Thurow's insights on the global economy; or hear award-winning actress, scholar, and playwright Anna Devere Smith's insights on race; or listen to former Gov. Mario Cuomo's views on building communities. We hope to see all of you in Orlando at the AASA National Conference, Feb. 14-17, 1997.

This past year, courage was also evident from the work that many of you did to support our work with Congress on the fiscal 1997 budget. What a turnaround! Less than two years ago, education was facing draconian cuts from a then-popular Congress. Just a few weeks ago, that same Congress passed a budget that increased education funding by $3.5 billion, the largest increase for education in years! Why? Of course, it was election-year politics. However, Congress only does things in election years that representatives perceive are popular politically. What is clear is that you, and your state and national organizations, have been very successful in reminding the American people that education represents the future of this country, and it must be supported. As we face future battles about such issues as vouchers, or the protection of children, we should be buoyed by knowing that we can get our message across to the public, and the public will respond.

A large part of understanding who we are is looking at our mission. In this spirit, the AASA Executive Committee recently took a fresh look at AASA's mission, adopting a new mission statement. It reads: "The mission of the American Association of School Administrators is to achieve the highest quality of public education through effective school system leadership, with emphasis on superintendents."

This was developed to help staff focus on the tasks at hand and to direct our limited resources and capacity toward the most important issues. There are several major ideas in the statement. First, we are focused on public education and efforts to make it of the highest quality. Second, our emphasis is on system leadership. In fact, AASA is the only national organization with a focus on system leadership. Finally, our internal emphasis is on superintendents. More than half of our members have historically been, and continue to be, superintendents.

Unfortunately, the last part of the mission statement has caused some uneasiness, because to some it appears to be exclusionary. These things are always in the eye of the beholder, but I choose to put a different spin on it. I believe that our emphasis, as an organization aimed at system leadership, is on the team that comprises the entire "superintendency," and I hope all those who are on that team can find a home at AASA. We believe we speak to your needs and your future. Obviously, the superin-tendency has a captain called the superintendent, who has some unique needs and challenges, and we must continue to focus on supporting those individuals as the centers of the team. Further, we have historically recruited and supported those individuals who plan to move into the superintendency in the future.

AASA hasn't changed its mission as much as we have tried to spotlight what we are about. I'm sure this will continue to be discussed by the Executive Committee, and I know they would welcome your comments and suggestions.

Who are we? Why are we here? We are people of courage and conviction. We are people open to new ideas and varied viewpoints. We are people capable of engaging others in the mission. And we keep our eyes on the ball. We are leaders.

Time to look at the results of the last national election in this century. Just what will the "bridge to the 21st century" look like, and will it be safe to cross? The best results of the election were that education and children emerged as issues unlikely to fade any time soon. And we now know that school leaders have a potentially powerful voice in shaping events.

࡚

Election Points to Power, Peril of Education's Politics

N ow that the smoke has cleared from the election, we need to assess where education stands. I was out of the country just before and during the election; I highly recommend that sort of distancing. What seems so important here loses its significance from afar. Also, you don't have to listen to all those silly political commercials and pumped-up punditry.

The election presented potential promise and peril for education. Democrats kept the White House and Republicans the Congress. With President Clinton acting unpredictably on various children's issues, a lot will hinge on whether Secretary Riley continues or is replaced. Riley has proven himself a stalwart defender of public education, and a friend of children and school leaders. If he does step down, hope that his replacement is cut from the same cloth; otherwise we could be in for some rough times. I am not confident that President Clinton is committed to the same values as his current secretary.

Congress tightened up between the two parties, but Republicans maintained control. That means we still have Newt and Co. to deal with at that end of Pennsylvania Avenue. The retirement of moderates from both parties probably will hurt education, since our issues tend to be settled in the middle of the political spectrum. However, the moderates who are left have much more power because if they defect to the other party, the game swings. A couple of dozen moderate Republicans have the power to soften the radical agenda we saw pursued in the last two years. At the same time, the turnover of key staff members dilutes institutional memory—always a moderating force. Bottom line, things on the Hill could be volatile.

The fact that Congress threw a lot of money at education at the 11th hour of the campaign probably saved a number of incumbents' jobs. They could truthfully explain back home that they had not lowered spending for schools, even though they had been trying to do so for 21 months. Whether the lesson they learned is that you shouldn't harm children and that you should support education, or that you can do anything you please until the election heats up, remains to be seen.

The good news from the election is that education is clearly on the minds of the voters. Both parties used education change as a theme, although their visions differed. Choice was embraced by both parties, as were charters. Public funding for private schools was part of the Republican platform. While the Democrats opposed it, President Clinton appeared to do one of his patented waffles in the first debate by stating that it was a local issue. He did make education a centerpiece of his campaign, although many of the ideas dealt with higher education.

Virtually all the major education issues voted on state-by-state were decided in our favor. Major bond issues were passed in a number of states, while the parental rights amendment went down in Colorado, and Oklahoma passed an initiative allowing superintendents to have multi-year contracts. Oregon did pass a funding rollback and the controversial affirmative action limitation passed in California, but all in all it was a good year for education issues.

The promise of the election was that the American public clearly wants to see schools get better and in many cases is prepared to pay to get better schools. The peril is that by being out in front, we make a good target. Clearly, the public has a short attention span and a low tolerance for disappointment. How long we can enjoy support is questionable; if we fail to deliver improvement, we can expect the worst.

Two issues should concern us. First, while we have held off the forces of private school choice, it is becoming a battle that is increasingly difficult to fight, particularly at the national level. The perception that many of our children, particularly in low-income areas, are attending schools that are unsafe and ineffective has increased the pressure for a radical solution.

While there are strong and persuasive public policy arguments against giving up on public education, the increasingly narrow—sometimes selfish—view that we should save a few of the children (especially my own) seems to be gaining credibility. We are going to have to generate some powerful, practical alternatives for improving education in the inner cities, or vouchers will surely be upon us.

The other issue that continues to dog us is the negative perception of school administrators. We often have been a favorite scapegoat, but I sense an emerging coalition of forces inside and outside of the profession whose members appear to be sharpening their axes. While the sky may not be falling, you can expect some significant chunks of debris in the months ahead.

What does all this mean? The need and the opportunity for leadership is greater than ever. Improving our schools and the lives of our children must remain our top priority. While we have to trust in God, it is a good idea to keep our powder dry. On the political scene, in Washington and in the state capitals, words from constituents on the home front will be more important than ever in influencing what Congress and legislatures do. School leaders have a tremendous opportunity to influence the future by shaping the opinions and actions of local supporters.

As former House speaker Tip O'Neill said, all politics is local. You are positioned to have tremendous influence. Use it, or lose it.

School leadership is one of the most relentless and sometimes thankless jobs around. Given that, it is easy to forget why we went into it and also easy to lose our sense of purpose and our will to continue. But I contend that we are called to this exquisite challenge.

ॐ

Building Cathedrals—That's What It's All About

E ducators are blessed. Every year we can celebrate two new years. One is the holiday; the other is the beginning of the school year. Each one gives us an opportunity to reflect on important questions and why we are doing what we are doing. The new year of 1997 will bring the usual quota of wonderful horrors that make up the lives of educational leaders. It also gives us a chance to once again question what we are about.

There is an old novelty song, which was popular years ago, sung from the perspective of one of General Custer's soldiers before the final engagement with Sitting Bull. The plaintive refrain sung by the soldier was "Gee

Mr. Custer, I don't want to go." He ended with the question most of us in school leadership face on a regular basis, which is, "What am I doin' here?"

A new year will bring continued attacks on us and the institutions we lead, and continued neglect by the broader public of the children we serve. So we probably are asking ourselves what we are doing here and thinking that perhaps we don't want to go anywhere but home to bed.

I will share a story that is set during medieval times. It concerns a man who, while walking through the forest one day, comes upon a great many men who are obviously engaged in building something. Each is armed with a hammer and chisel. The man goes up to one fellow and asks him what he is doing. "I'm carving stone," he replies. While the answer was truthful, it didn't add much to the gentleman's understanding of what was happening.

He approaches yet another worker and poses the same question. The second worker replies that he is carving stone to build a building. Now the traveler is getting closer to the answer but he is still confused, so he approaches yet another worker and asks him what he is doing. That worker answers, "Why, I'm carving stone to build a building. In fact, the building will be a cathedral. It will rise hundreds of feet into the air and will stand for hundreds of years. Thousands will flock here to worship God and to connect with their highest possible purpose."

At one level, each of these workers was doing the same job. They were carving stone. Yet the vision they held for their work was very different. We need to constantly ask ourselves what the vision is that we have for our work. Are we building cathedrals or just chopping away at rock?

If you became an educator or a school administrator because you were looking for a good job, you are in serious need of career counseling. Or you might think you have the easiest job in town because everyone seems to know how to do it better than you, or that is the impression they give at board meetings or in letters to the editor. But anyone who thinks a great job is one that requires long hours with lots of criticism and little praise; which, when carried out with high integrity and passion may be cause for dismissal; which has maximum responsibility with minimum authority; and which has the job security of a nervous bomb squad de-fuser, is someone who needs professional help. This is a terrible job and a horrible way to make a living!

But, it is a good way to live because it is not a job nearly so much as it is a mission. School leadership in today's world isn't a job, it's a calling. It's an opportunity for service and for helping others. It gives you the chance to impact the lives of hundreds or thousands of children. It lets you put your finger on the scales of justice to tip them, just a bit, in favor of those who have been unfavored. It allows you to knit together the unraveled fabric of your community so that a web of support is made possible. It allows you to transform institutions and the lives that those institutions touch. Most importantly, it allows you to nurture hopes and dreams.

Zorba the Greek said "What a strange machine man is! You fill him with bread, wine, fish and radishes, and out come sighs, laughter and dreams." Jobs have to do with bread and radishes; missions have to do with laughter and dreams. Our mission is to keep the laughter alive and the dreams burning in the hearts of our children.

In our work, it is easy to get caught up in the mechanics. We deal with standards and goals and assessments. We confront bonds and buildings and buses. We are bombarded with editorials and erudition. It is very easy to get sidetracked and to lose our perspective. That is why so many of us spend so much of our time sick at heart and wondering what we are doing here.

It is important to remember that our work isn't a science nearly so much as it is an art. It is tough work tending to the human spirit. But that, more than anything else, is what our work is about. In the movie "Mr. Smith Goes to Washington," just as Mr. Smith is leaving to take his place in Congress, his father reminds him that the only causes worth fighting for are lost causes. Lost causes are the ones that deal with the human journey towards the highest possibilities. It is easy to do hard things. It is much harder to do the right things, and yet, that is what our work is about. It is doing the right things for those who are not yet ready to do these things for themselves.

What are we doing here, in this new year? Why, we are building cathedrals of the human spirit. Not a bad life at all, when we remember what it's really about. Happy New Year!

ॐ

Being a school leader is like being an electrician. We deal with power; it's a bit dangerous; and we have to make sure all the wires connect correctly so that flow is maintained. Given our challenges, maybe it's time to rewire the whole enterprise.

ॐ

To Spark Improvement, Make the Connections

The National Conference on Education© had many lessons for us as school leaders. I'm not only talking about the ones learned in the sessions or in our casual conversations around the reception circuit. When I became executive director, one major goal was to have the AASA National Conference on Education become the major national educational event of the year. One that, if you attended, would provide you with an experience you could not find anywhere else.

Our goal was to provide a strong mix of outstanding and provocative, insightful General Session speakers, substantial Distinguished Lecturers and hands-on help in our small sessions. We also wanted to provide focal points that would address the myriad concerns of school leaders as we near the 21st century: concerns as wide ranging as the condition of children, leadership and career advancement. "Kids in the Spotlight," "Leadership on the Line," and the "Jobs Central" strands helped fill that bill.

We strove to infuse the conference with intellectual content and personal joy. We wanted you to go home refilled and refreshed. From all accounts, we have indeed made the conference the special event of the year, and I suggest you put Feb. 27-March 2, 1998, on your calendar so you can join us in San Diego — our most popular conference city.

But what I wanted to share with you was not a review of the specifics, as great as they might be; that's not what made the conference a special event. Many national conferences have great specific pieces. What is special about the AASA National Conference is that we model for you what the job of leadership is in today's world—providing a holistic, coherent interconnection of ideas and programs.

I believe that much of the current discussion on school improvement and school reform misses the mark badly—not because the ideas are wrong, but because they are disconnected and lack a sense of clarity and purpose. Education is not a collection of parts, it is a whole process that must make sense to people. Disjointed and unconnected events and activities have disjointed and unconnected outcomes. It is only through combining efforts and tying them together that synergy is achieved. The whole really is greater than the sum of the parts.

Further, education is not a machine that can be repaired a part at a time. You cannot "fix" education because a fix implies a mechanical solution. We can tinker on the tractor until "the cows come home and the rooster crows," and the tinkering will not make the kinds of improvements we want to see. That is because we have to improve the entire barnyard and all the livestock in it. The tractor is merely a means of raising the crops to feed the animals. The whole cannot be fixed in parts. Education cannot be reformed a piece at a time. The parts and all the connections linking the parts have to be improved simultaneously.

Education is not mechanical. It is organic. Because it is a system made up of living, breathing organisms (children, teachers, administrators, parents, community members, etc.), it must be viewed as an organic entity whose parts are interconnected. When one part of our body is ill, the whole body suffers, and the treatment must take that into consideration. You can't cure a broken arm by cutting it off the body and giving it "staff development." You can't "site-base" an inflamed leg. Treatment of the whole patient is required— calcium to build the bones, antibiotics to reduce the infection.

Leadership in today's organizations (note the root word of "organization" is "organ") must come from those who understand that all of the parts are important and must be interwoven into a whole piece. Leadership is "sense-making" for those in the organization. Leaders must make the connections for people so they understand the whole and how they relate to it. You cannot galvanize the members of an organization to do only their part and expect the organization to perform at its peak. Folks need to know how the pieces fit together and that they, in fact, do fit together.

School reform will not occur until those of us leading the effort see that you can't fix the individual pieces separately and expect things to get better. Leadership is that role that connects the parts to create a whole. School reform must come from a comprehensive understanding and holistic view of a very complex and interwoven enterprise known as teaching and learning.

Similarly, the National Conference on Education© is not just a collection of interesting parts. It is a total experience tied together by overarching themes and strands. Our role as leader is to identify the themes of our organizations and create the strands that bind them into a coherent whole.

One other aspect of our conference, which I have gotten a lot of positive feedback from, is the "talk show" format at the beginning of our General Sessions. We invite a few guests to sit and discuss the theme of the day.

This does several things. First, it allows us to do the obligatory greetings in a more interesting way. But beyond that, it again offers the opportunity to help make sense of the experience and put it in context. Most importantly, it models the interactive quality necessary for today's leader. The days of commanding attention and talking at folks are over. Engagement and interaction are the tools of the modern leader. We can't talk at, we must talk with; today's leaders don't give the answers, they raise the questions.

Many of you know my fondness for Yogi Berra quotes. One of my favorites is: "You can observe a lot just by watching." I would add Houston's corollary, which is: "You can hear a lot, just by listening." Our role in the future is to listen and then lead by making a coherent whole out of the disparate parts.

៛

Sometimes I just have to rant. As I watched the push for higher standards move from a good idea to religious dogma, I felt compelled to put in my two cents' worth. There is nothing wrong, and a lot right, with setting high expectations for learning. But there is a great deal wrong with blindly doing so without considering the challenges involved.

ॐ

More Than Good Coaching Needed To Cross 'Standards' Finish Line

Standards. Higher standards. World-class standards. Standards have become the mantra of school reform. They have replaced apple pie and motherhood as the one thing no educator can be against. On the surface this makes sense. A recent study by the Public Agenda Foundation found that students today do not feel they are being held to a high enough standard of performance. The literature is replete with information on grade inflation, low expectations for minority students and a raft of other subjects that would indicate that holding students to a much higher set of expectations for their work makes great sense. In my conversations with teachers, school leaders and with citizens, all seem to agree that higher standards are a must.

Yet, at the risk of pointing out that the emperor's clothes are a bit thread-bare, I must raise the caution flag on the standards movement. Not because higher standards are wrong, but because the movement itself is flawed. If we ever expect to reach a higher set of outcomes for students, we'd better fix the movement that we expect to take us there.

Let's start with the assumptions undergirding the reform movement. It is widely reported, and therefore believed by politicians and the business community, that American education has slipped badly in recent years. Starting with the pivotal "A Nation at Risk" report of 1983, it has been taken for granted that the golden era of American public education is behind us, that we have lost the competitive edge over the rest of the world, and that our economic future is threatened by a decline in the quality of education in America.

It would take more than a few paragraphs to refute this claim. However, let it be known that there is a substantial body of evidence that our schools have held their own against a rising tide of social problems. Despite the dramatic decline in family life, and overall loss of social capital supporting children, schools have maintained and slightly increased achievement. While most international comparisons are bogus, at best, because of different samples, curricular assumptions and cultural variances, when comparisons are made with like groups, the United States does just fine.

We do need to improve what we are doing, though, and improve it dramatically, because incremental improvement will not suffice in an exponential environment. Expectations for all children have skyrocketed against the past and we have not kept up with those expectations. So improvement is needed. But not for the reasons the critics assume. And if we have misdiagnosed the problem, we are quite likely to prescribe the wrong treatment. A blind call for higher standards without examining what children need to know how to do better could well lead to wasted time and resources.

The second problem with the standards movement is that it fails to consider context as a powerful issue. Having served as a superintendent of a wealthy district, where most children came from two-parent families with high levels of parental income and education (not to mention expectations), and having served as a superintendent of a couple of urban districts with high levels of poverty and "broken" families, it is difficult for me to take the standards movement seriously absent a consideration of the contextual differences the children bring to school with them.

I am not for a moment suggesting that poor children should not have the opportunity to meet the same high expectations that wealthier children are expected to meet. In fact, it is our moral imperative to see that the trajectories of their lives have the same opportunity for liftoff. I am suggesting a school reform movement that does not consider the problems presented by lack of equity—that suggests all students reach the same finish line but does nothing to redress the fact that the starting line is further back for some—is a movement that I have difficulty taking seriously. Thus far, I have seen nothing from the politicians of either party that would indicate that we can expect this issue to be confronted and addressed. Without dealing with context, the standards movement is doomed to fail.

The fact is, we already have high standards for some children. Students who attend our highly selective and competitive magnet high schools in some of our inner cities . . . schools such as Stuyvesant and the Bronx High School of Science in New York, or University High in Tucson, Ariz., or the dozens of others all across America, meet and exceed the world-class standards that are currently being discussed. Students attending many of our elite suburban schools also meet these standards. The consortium in the Chicago area that outstripped the world on the recent TIMSS study is evidence of that. Our problem isn't that American students can't meet higher standards. The problem is that we lack the will as a people to do what we have to do to see that all students have the same opportunities that some of our children have.

Another problem I have with the standards movement is that it is totally disconnected from everything else we do. Education is organic. It is fluid. It lives and breathes because, of all the aspects of our existence, it is perhaps the most human and the most dependent upon humans to carry out. Those acting and those acted upon are human. And as the old saying points out, "You can lead a horse to water, but you can't make him drink." You can lead a student to knowledge, but you can't make him learn. That requires motivation, understanding and sometimes compassion. It is the stuff of hopes and dreams. And it will take more than a mantra to fulfill. It will take fairness and equity. It will take strength and joy. It will take us acting toward each other in human ways. It will take our behaving in connected ways.

And finally, we must ask, "Higher standards for whom?" For if we want to have higher standards for students, we must also have higher standards for teachers. And if we want to hold teachers to higher standards, we must do the same for principals. And what is good for principals is good for district staff and superintendents. And that leads to higher standards for boards of education, which naturally leads to parents and community. For good measure, let's throw in business leaders and politicians. Children are at the bottom of the food chain. Blaming them for their problems and not taking responsibility as adults for adding to their problems is really blaming the victim. Yes, children need to reach high standards. So do adults.

If the emperor wants to show off his new duds, he needs to make sure everyone is dressed as well. When we can truly begin to understand what our kids need to know and know what to do to face an uncertain future, when we can see that all our kids have the same chance at success that is currently reserved for a few of our kids, when we can connect all the parts of education and join together—adults and children working toward the same end of higher achievement—then we can all start chanting the mantra together. It will be more than a mystical incantation, it will be a goal within our grasp.

∂❧

The need for civility and responsibility in all of us is greater today than at any time in our history. As our society has become more complex and diverse, the need to learn to get along and help each other has gotten greater. Unfortunately, we are also seeing a greater emphasis on the individual and more narrow interests. How we resolve this tension will say much about what we as a country become in the next century. And as usual, the schools are right in the middle of the action.

ॐ

Students Are Valuable Resources, Not Problems To Be Solved

At times it appears that our society is running a race between its best intentions and its worst instincts. Lately, we have seen and heard a lot about a greater need for civility and caring in America. Many fear that we are coming apart as a nation and that unless we get back to a sense of caring for each other, we may be lost.

There has been and continues to be a real tension between our private instincts, our "pursuit of happiness" — to use the phrase from the Declaration of Independence — and our public spirit, which undergirds the possibility of our preserving "life and liberty" in a democratic society.

Public education came about because people like Horace Mann understood that a democracy depended on a public making informed decisions dedicated to the common good. That cannot happen with each person only taking care of his or her own narrow circle.

The fact of modern America — which far too often gets lost in the rush toward our most narrow self-interests — is that we are all in this one together, whether we like it or not. As Martin Luther King Jr. reminded us, "What affects one of us affects all of us." We cannot build our walls high enough or thick enough to protect ourselves and our own children from the effects of other's children.

AASA recently has been involved in two events that I hope will allow more people to embrace civic-mindedness as an essential goal of public education.

Last month, AASA joined with more than 30 organizations in signing a "Declaration on Education and a Civil Society" and then participated with hundreds of additional groups in making a commitment to youth as part of the Presidents' Summit for America's Future.

The Declaration is the first step in a 10-year plan to integrate civic values into every aspect of the educational experience and "weave a seamless web between school and community." The promise of the Declaration, though, is in its recognition of youth as resources to be tapped, rather than problems to be solved.

"Young people need to see themselves as leaders, not victims," says Harris Wofford, a former U.S. Senator and CEO of the Corporation for National Service. Therefore, a primary goal of the Partnering Initiative on Education and Civil Society is to expand service learning opportunities for our youth.

There has been some controversy over whether children should be required to do community service, and reasonable people can disagree on that point. Yet while only one state — Maryland — currently mandates service as a graduation requirement, countless schools and districts are witnessing the benefits — for students, schools and communities — of expanding service opportunities and integrating them with curricula. The goal of the partnering initiative is to expand the number of organizations involved by establishing 10,000 partner schools in the next 10 years to serve as resource centers.

It's simple. If we — parents, schools, communities, churches — don't teach goodness, how else are children going to learn it? Kids don't know what they don't know. You have to expose them to the opportunity to serve, so they can find out if it is something they should do. Not every child will walk away from a required bout of service with a sense of needing to contribute, but many will. I would argue many more than would come to it out of instinct.

God knows, the need in our communities for helping hands, minds and hearts is great.

Perhaps even more compelling for school administrators trying to run safe, orderly schools that graduate lifelong learners, though, is the positive impact service learning has in developing thinkers, doers and problem solvers, rather than passive students who at their best are only worried about grades and test scores. Service learning can offer various leadership opportunities to suit the diverse gifts and talents that make up school enrollments today.

Raysa Santos, a 9th grader who might be labeled "at-risk" in another context, sums up the value of service as an educational opportunity. Says Santos, who volunteers as part of her personalized education plan at the Metropolitan Career and Technical Center in Providence, R.I.: "I appreciate . . . having real responsibilities and deadlines to meet. It helps me to be motivated when I get up in the morning . . . to know that I have real work to do."

Beyond requiring our children to provide service to the community, though, we must recognize that we are still the adults—the parents, teachers, mentors — in the picture. We must provide models for students of what it means to serve.

Several years ago, I called for all adults to see themselves as shepherds for our children — caring for them and helping them find their way. That's why we are excited by the many commitments made by various organizations represented at the Summit — from community groups to businesses — to help answer the needs of youth in our communities.

AASA itself will be a major partner in follow-up activities, because Summit organizers apparently recognize the pivotal role superintendents can play in bringing communities together around children's issues.

"Goodness, Justice and Excellence — Foundation for Education." That's the theme AASA President Karl Hertz has chosen for the coming year. It's a theme that sums up eloquently the link between service, learning and continuing to build on our great democracy. Perhaps the Summit in Philadelphia and the Declaration on Education and Civil Society will provide the spark for a new American revolution that builds on those hopes penned over 200 years ago in Philadelphia — that we have a nation where we pursue "life, liberty and happiness" as a "people" with joint responsibility for each other. That is how we will preserve our greatness for our children.

ð

School superintendents have historically played a pivotal role in communities. Over the last several decades, however, the respect associated with the role has diminished and its centrality has eroded. With the increased attention being given to the issues of children and the disconnection of communities, we have an historic opportunity to move back to the center of the action. The America's Promise Campaign, led by General Colin Powell, furthers that opportunity.

ঽ৶

Summit Calls Superintendents to Front, Center

In last month's column, I mentioned the Summit for America's Future, sponsored by President Clinton and the living former presidents, and chaired by Gen. Colin Powell. AASA's then President Don Thompson, President-Elect Karl Hertz and I were fortunate enough to be among a limited number of educators invited to the conference. There was considerable good news in the conference. Although the media reports spotlighted the emphasis of the meeting on the issue of volunteerism, the real issue of the conference was children, especially those children who are most at risk in our society. This was clearly Gen. Powell's priority. He repeated this theme throughout the Summit. Further, every session I attended focused on education as the centerpiece for solving the problems of America. There was a great deal of discussion about the reform agenda for America's schools and about support for helping schools get better. The other major positive theme was that the conference was so bipartisan. As Karl Hertz pointed out recently at his installation, children are not a Republican issue or a Democratic issue, a liberal issue or a conservative issue, they are a human issue. That was clear in the broad spectrum of people attending, and from the makeup of the panels, which featured prominent people from both parties, from all ends of the political spectrum. Indeed, America may at last be ready to do something for its children and set politics aside.

However, there was also some bad news evident in the conference. First, there was a fair amount of cynicism, both inside the meetings and outside on the streets. Inside, there were those who clearly are using the issue of volunteerism and children to advance their own narrow agenda and personal goals. Outside, the meeting was criticized by the extremes at both ends of the political spectrum. Those on the right pronounced it as but one more attempt by big brother to take over the lives of Americans. The left saw it as a cop-out — an attempt to replace government responsibility with volunteerism.

In fact, if you listened carefully, it was clear that the Summit positioned itself directly in the middle. It was repeatedly pointed out that our tradition in this country has been based on a common acceptance of a mutual responsibility for one another, and that volunteerism goes back to our founding days. It was also repeatedly emphasized that there are problems so great and so severe that they can only be solved through our collective will, which must be exerted through government action. I was particularly struck by one panel member who suggested that, while the meeting centered at Independence Hall, we should consider changing its name to "Interdependence Hall." The name more clearly describes our national character of the past, and the real solution to our present and future challenges.

Although education was the centerpiece of the discussion, educators were not front and center in the discussion. While some of the education groups from Washington were present, such as AASA, many were not.

While a number of the cities had included educators and superintendents on their teams, many others did not. Virtually none of the discussion panels had educators on them, including the education panel! Once again, we were not in the loop.

Although there was much discussion about the need for education reform, much of that talk was off-target, with often simplistic and naive assumptions about what the problems are and how to solve them. This might have something to do with the fact that few educators were directly involved in the planning and execution of the meeting.

While the conference demonstrated our diversity as a nation, by virtue of its makeup and the various perspectives presented, it was also clear that there is no common thrust for what we should be doing. Thus, the strategies for achieving the goals of the Summit could become fragmented and lose their potential power. Also, there were many promises made. It will be much more difficult to see if they will be kept.

The really good news to come out of the conference for AASA, and for school leaders, is the leadership role we have been asked to play in the follow up. AASA will serve as a convener for 100 mini-summits strategically located to involve more than 90 percent of the communities in the country. This thrusts local superintendents right where we belong, in the center of the community of support for children.

While it does take a village to raise a child, it takes leadership to raise a village, and it will require your leadership to make America's Promise (the name given to the organization that will lead the Summit follow-up activities), America's reality. We are often frustrated by being left out. This will allow us to act on what we know must be done for children, rather than react to what others think needs to be done.

Once again, I felt compelled to say, "hold on here, partner, we're getting carried away" when I saw everyone from the President on down doing an end-zone victory dance about the latest results from the Third International Math and Science Study, which had America near the top of the heap. It's all right to celebrate some welcome good news, but a great deal about the testing story should still worry us. So let's save some of the dancing for the Super Bowl.

ॐ

Celebrate Achievement, Not Scores

Educators have been heartened by the recent results of the Third International Math and Science Study (better known as TIMMS), which show that American students are above average in both math and science. In fact, U.S. 4th grade students ranked second only to Korea in science and ranked near the top in math.

I must admit it was great to see headlines stating that American students "soared" on international tests. It would be quite easy to celebrate and pat ourselves on the back because we have had little to cheer about in terms of how our performance has been reported in the press.

It is not that we haven't done well before. A study several years ago showed American 3rd graders second in the world in reading. You might not have known that, and it is quite likely your communities didn't know it, because it was barely noted by the press. In fact, previous good news has been consistently relegated to the back pages of the papers, so we can be forgiven for feeling good about seeing good news prominently displayed. However, I would like to raise some cautionary thoughts.

First, most of us know how little achievement tests really tell us about what children are doing. We know, for example, that the mismatch of curriculum to tests, the skewed test sampling and even the mathematics tend to distort the information. American students often don't perform as well on international comparisons as other students simply because our curriculum is different. It is difficult to do well on an algebra exam if you haven't taken algebra. Further, America tends to educate a larger portion of its population (and subsequently tests a larger portion of its children) than many other countries. Because larger samples lower results, we often get criticized for drops in scores when those drops are meaningless.

The fact that we now test nearly half of our high school students on the SAT as compared to a much smaller sample in previous years has led to great alarm as the average has dropped. No one wants to consider that students who make C's in high school don't perform as well as those who make A's; therefore, when more C students are tested you naturally get a decline in the average. That America has opened college admission to a much broader portion of our population should be a point of celebration, not criticism, because students who at one time would never have taken the test are now taking it in order to further their education.

In fact, despite testing greater percentages of students, and despite a decline in the conditions affecting their performance, which is outside of the schools' control, we have seen some improvements in test scores in recent years. I suggest that, rather than celebrating that, a better response might be "so what?"

I am not suggesting that we should not feel good about what we are doing, or that we shouldn't try to set the critics straight. What I am suggesting is that we use extreme caution in getting too wrapped up in the whole testing craze.

America has a scoreboard mentality, which leads us to want to know who is No. 1. Yet we must remember we are in the business of dealing with individuals. Do comparisons among unique individuals make sense? Ranking countries or schools or children is not only distorting the truth mathematically, it is degrading to the people involved. Yes, we should know how well we are doing and progressing—that's why criterion-referenced tests were invented. But rank ordering people doesn't tell us anything.

Moreover, can we test what is truly important? Is there an Iowa Test of Basic Courage or a Stanford Test for Compassion? We all know that most of what is important in what we do in school, as well as what we do in life, cannot be reduced to a paper-and-pencil assessment in which we fill in bubbles of finite information. Life is not a game of Jeopardy nor is it a trivial pursuit. We must be careful to keep the important things important.

Because of the political realities that we face, I see far too many of us falling into the testing trap laid by those who want everything reduced to a score sheet. We promise that all the kids will be at grade level or above average or whatever. This longing for Lake Wobegone (where all the men are strong, the women beautiful and the children above average), not only fails to distinguish between the different kinds of assessment and what each kind can really tell us, but it also places the emphasis on the most trivial elements of what we do in school. Leadership requires us to remind those who are calling for "accountability" to place the accountability on the right things. Yes, we have to let the public know how well we are performing. Let's get a bit more creative with what it is we report and a bit more forceful in standing up to challenge stupid reporting.

Finally, while it is good to note when test results are up, we must also understand that there will be results that are not so good. We have always done better in the lower grades than the upper ones. It might be interesting to try to figure out why that is. More child-centered learning and a more integrated curriculum? Learning that takes place in smaller, more personal environments? Fewer outside distractions like jobs, dating and

MTV? A greater cumulative effect of the American culture that de-emphasizes the value of learning? Whatever. The fact is that some scores will be up and some down, and we must remember as we rush to celebrate the highs that the lows will surely come. If you live by the scores, you'll die by the scores.

America seems to have a hard time dealing with the obvious. Poor kids have a harder time learning than kids who aren't poor. Schools with lots of poor kids have more difficulty helping kids succeed than those with fewer poor kids. If we want to improve American education, we have to start with the obvious.

ક⁀

School Leaders in High-Poverty Districts Have Three Strikes Against Them

In this season of baseball, I was thinking recently of the old favorite, "Casey at the Bat." You remember that tale about how the town of Mudville pinned its hopes on mighty Casey to pull their team through. But Casey disappointed them by striking out. This reminded me of how we, as school leaders, are often seen as disappointments to our own communities. This story seemed particularly apt as I recently looked over a report that has been submitted to Congress concerning the use of Chapter 1 money and poor children. As a part of the Elementary and Secondary Education Act, Congress required that the analysis be done. The results of that study are disturbing on several fronts and can cause little joy in Mudville or elsewhere.

The analysis, referred to as "Prospects," was designed to compare the educational achievement of those children with significant participation in Chapter 1 programs with comparable children who did not receive Chapter 1. It was also to examine a range of cognitive, behavioral and affective outcome measures such as achievement, truancy, delinquency and school dropout rates, employment and earnings, and enrollment in secondary education.

The analysis was done between high-poverty schools (where at least 75 percent of the children come from poverty) and low-poverty schools. It will come as no surprise to most to find that there is a significant learning gap between high- and low-poverty schools. Large differences in reading and math achievement exist at each grade level. This is particularly true of higher-order skills. Students in low-poverty schools score between 50 and 75 percent higher in reading and math. And that gap seems to widen as the students progress through school.

Further, students in high-poverty schools get lower grades, have higher absenteeism and are suspended more. This is also reflected (or perhaps caused?) by the teachers' opinions of these students, which are also lower. Contributing factors might include the fact that these students are more likely to live in single-parent homes and in homes with low family incomes, to be on welfare, and to live in homes where the parent is less likely to have completed high school and more likely to speak a language other than English.

Further, high-poverty schools have higher transfer rates and larger classes. Although these schools have more staff, which no doubt reflects the higher number of special programs available in these schools, other studies have shown that these schools tend to have teachers who are less experienced and more likely to be teaching subjects they are not qualified to teach. Strike one is that poor kids in schools with high numbers of like students have many problems to face, both inside and outside of school.

Strike two is the lack of success in off-setting these problems. Chapter 1 doesn't seem to make that much difference. The achievement gap remains for students in Chapter 1 programs. The gains were no better than matched control groups. And a sizable portion of the students needing help are not getting it. What this means is that there are not enough resources to help all the kids who need it and the resources being used are not having enough impact.

Strike three involves the fact that the real variable is the concentration of poverty. The problems in American education are clearly located in those schools with the highest concentrations of poor children. The problems are greater and the school response is often weakest. And while the problems of poverty fall hardest on poor children, in schools where there are large concentrations of poor children, all children suffer. Schools that serve poor students tend to have less to spend and are more likely to have inadequate heating and plumbing, as well as older books and insufficient supplies and equipment.

Further, recent brain research raises real questions about our priorities. We, as a nation, are spending billions to offset the effects of poverty but we have spread it around and are using it perhaps too late to have an impact. This raises very troubling policy questions. Should we be spreading extra resources for every poor child across the country when it seems clear that poor children in schools that do not have high concentrations of poverty seem to be doing well and are receiving greater resources anyway? Further, if most of the kids' wiring for learning is set by the age of three, why aren't we spending money at that level first, rather than remediating later?

Even raising these questions, much less answering them, causes great political peril. However, if we are ever to expect any joy in Mudville, mighty Casey has got to step up to the plate and takes his cuts. Otherwise, we, as school leaders, will get called out on strikes without even swinging the bat.

Articles *of* Faith & Hope *for* Public Education

Section II:

Additional Thoughts

I get truly tired of people who should know better using the schools as a scapegoat that I must rebel and "take back the streets." Joe Schneider, who is now deputy executive director of AASA and who co-wrote *Exploding the Myths* with me, collaborated in taking former Secretary of Education Bill Bennett down a few pegs with this piece that appeared in the *Phi Delta Kappan* magazine.

કે

Drive-By Critics and Silver Bullets

At some point, school administrators need to say, "Enough is enough. We're not going to put up with school-bashing any more. Get your facts straight, you scornful critics, or find yourselves a new patsy."

As public servants, we come by our thick skin naturally. So it's not surprising that we quietly endure blast after blast at our so-called lousy public schools. Most administrators are willing to take on critics of their own school or school district. But that gives the loudmouths with access to a national forum the opportunity to go unchallenged when they lump all public schools together before trashing them.

Nobody does this better than William Bennett. While President Reagan's second secretary of education, he used the federal post as a "bully pulpit" from which to denounce the evils of public education. And he's been preaching the same sermon since leaving office. Common sense would suggest that the nation's media would by now be immune to Bennett's tirades. Today, a "Bennett Blasts Quality of Public Education" article would seem to be about as newsworthy as a "dog bites man" story. Alas, the media love pit bull stories, and nobody chews on education with more tenacity than Bill Bennett. Consequently, his latest ankle-biting attack grabbed front-page headlines in newspapers throughout the country.

Bennett teamed up with Emily Feistritzer, one of his favorite data collectors, to produce what they call *The Report Card on American Education 1993*. Bennett's own Empower American organization and something called the American Legislative Exchange Council (ALEC), which lists Bennett as a trustee of its foundation, paid the bills to get the report into the media's hands.

The report card purports to show which states are most effective at educating students. Guess what? The analysis suggests that those states with the highest student achievement tend to be states that don't spend much on education. Having "proved" this with selected facts and figures, Bennett concludes, "There is no correlation between increased spending on education and higher student achievement." Not one of his five highest-achieving states, he says, ranks in the top 25 in per-pupil expenditures.

Feistritzer's data also give Bennett the opportunity to suggest that something dramatic should be done about the condition of American education. His self-described most important recommendation for change? You guessed it: vouchers. "A reform agenda should allow parents to choose the public, private, or religious schools to which they send their children."

Overall, though, Bennett is fairly silent about solutions. The primary purpose of the report card, he says in his accompanying release, is not to prescribe solutions but to provide data by which"the American people can assess both the condition and the trends of American education. An honest assessment of the facts, after all, should be the starting point of policy debates."

On that point we're in agreement. But what bothers us is the way Bennett interprets, selects, drops, and adds data under the guise of conducting "an honest assessment."

For example, Bennett makes much of student scores on what was formerly called the Scholastic Aptitude Test (SAT) and on the college entrance test of the American College Testing (ACT) program. Despite repeated disclaimers by the developers of these tests and admonitions from every testing expert we know, Bill Bennett wants the public and the press to continue to regard these tests as measures of what schools teach and what students learn. In fact, the examinations are designed only to predict freshman success in college. Moreover, SAT and ACT questions are not now, nor have they every been, designed to measure what secondary schools teach.

Bennett ignores these well-established facts because he and other public school critics realize that the media jump on simple comparisons and easy-to-understand score data. Consequently, SAT and ACT scores become useful clubs with which to beat up public educators.

The problem for American education is that so much of the public and so many of the policymakers in this country have swallowed Bennett's message, hook, line, and assumption. Unfortunately, bad assumptions make bad policy. Put another way, if you lean your ladder against the wrong wall, you're going to paint the wrong house.

Let's spend a minute or two with the nation's report card that Feistritzer prepared and Bennett so enjoys sharing. It is a thing of massive proportions, containing a nearly infinite array of numbers. It provides a ranking of each state on a number of measures such as results on the National Assessment of Educational Progress (NAEP), ACT scores, SAT scores, school graduation rates, pupil/teacher ratios, expenditures, teacher salaries, per-capita income, percentage of poverty, and minority enrollment. Frankly, the rows and rows of numbers beg for an interpretation, and Bennett, of course, provides it. Smart approach. That way the public does not have to do the heavy lifting of figuring out for themselves how the numbers add up.

The entire analysis is done by rank ordering the states. Of course, ranking tends both to flatten data and to exaggerate differences. For example, the state with the greatest percentage of students with limited proficiency in English (not part of the information provided in Bennett's "most comprehensive report") is California. Over 28% of its students have limited proficiency in English. The state with the 10th-highest number of students with limited proficiency in English has 9% of its students in that category. Both of these are high numbers, but the number-one ranking state has three times more of these students than the number 10 state. The number-40 state, on the other hand, has only 1.5% of its students in the limited English proficiency category, while the number-50 state has .9%. Neither of these percentages is significant, yet we are talking about the spread between the 40th and 50th states in the ranking. In other words, the first and 10th states are dramatically different, but the difference among the 10 lowest-ranking states is minimal.

The numbers having to do with limited English proficiency figure into another part of the story that Bennett's data don't tell. That is, he makes much ado about his "top 10 states." So do the media when they report on the study. The states are Iowa, North Dakota, Minnesota, Nebraska, Wisconsin, Idaho, Utah, Wyoming, Kansas, and South Dakota. But only one, Minnesota, has any significant number of immigrant students or students who speak a language other than English at home. Even then, four of the other top states (North Dakota, South Dakota, Iowa, and Utah) actually lost immigrant school-age children during the last 10 years.

Poverty is another variable Bennett fails to factor into his figuring. Three of his top 10 states have fewer than 50,000 poor children statewide; none has more than 94,000. North Dakota, one of Bennett's best, has fewer than 20,000 poor children statewide and fewer than 900 students with limited proficiency in English.

Bennett's basic analysis is just as incomplete and just as flawed. He trumpets that "we have suffered a severe decline in education" over the last 20 years. And he uses test scores to make this argument. However, if we look at the wall chart itself, we find that the NAEP results he uses are for only one subject in one grade and for one year. Further, several states aren't even ranked because of problems with the test. Of the 42 states listed, 15 are said in the footnote of the report to have shown significantly higher scores than in the previous testing.

Bennett correctly points out that SAT scores have been on the decline since 1972. Back then the average score was 937, while in 1982 it was 893. This represents about a 3% decline, or about five fewer questions answered correctly. However, in 1993 the average had moved up to 902, so for the past 10 years the trend has been up, not down. Further, if one examines who took the test, the picture is even more revealing. Unfortunately, Bennett doesn't do that. We did, though. In 1982 about 26% of high school seniors took the test. In 1993 about 43% of them took it. In effect, a slight improvement occurred in the results of the test, even as a much larger slice of America's youth took it.

Bennett's lack of candor is most flagrant whenever he forces "expenditures" and "achievement" into the same sentence. He likes to point out, for example, that Utah, which is 51st in per-pupil expenditures, nevertheless ranks fourth on the SAT and 10th on the ACT. Now Utah is a fine place, full of wonderful people, but Bennett oversells is accomplishments. It seems to us that a state that has only 4% of its seniors taking the SAT *ought* to rank high in the ratings. When only 4% of the seniors take the SAT, you can bet that they represent Utah's finest.

If half of Utah's seniors took the SAT, we would expect the state's ranking to fall noticeably. Compare Utah to the District of Columbia, for example. On the SAT, the District's ranking among states is near the bottom. But consider this: 76% of seniors in the nation's capital take the SAT. That means a lot of students who didn't even enroll in college-prep courses are taking a test designed to measure how well they would perform in college. Had public schools in the District allowed only those students preparing to go on to college to take the SAT, the total number of test-takers would have declined dramatically, and the city's ranking among states would have shot upward.

So why don't more of Utah's students take the SAT? The answer is that Utah is one of those states where most students prefer to take the ACT. Even then, Utah ranks only 10th on the ACT list. All right, the 10th spot is still pretty good—it means that Utah did better than 40 other states and the District of Columbia, right? Well, not exactly. That kind of reasoning is just what Bennett wants from you. The fact is, only 27 states are ranked on Bennett's wall chart under the category of ACT results. Ranking 10th when the total is 27 is certainly far less spectacular than ranking 10th in a field of all 50 states and the District of Columbia.

Table 1 sheds a different light on Bennett's "top 10 achieving states." The table gives the state ranking by SAT scores, the state ranking based on the percentage of children in the state taking the SAT, and the state ranking based on the percentage of school-age children living in poverty. What the table demonstrates is that many of the high-scoring SAT states rank at or near the bottom of the states in terms of the percentage of children taking the test and have some of the fewest students living in poverty. Iowa, in other words, has the highest SAT scores. But only two other states have a smaller percentage of children taking the test. Similarly, only two other states have fewer children in poverty. It's worth keeping in mind that poverty is the single best predictor of how well a student will do on the SAT. Consequently, it's no surprise that states with little poverty and small numbers of SAT test-takers rank high on Bennett's wall chart.

TABLE 1. BENNETT'S TOP 10 STATES

	Ranking by SAT Score	Ranking by Percentage of Seniors Taking SAT	Ranking by Number of Students in Poverty
Iowa	1	49	49
N. Dakota	2	46	32
Minnesota	5	39	29
Nebraska	8	39	47
Wisconsin	7	39	30
Idaho	21	30	26
Utah	4	50	22
Wyoming	22	33	50
Kansas	6	42	37
S. Dakota	3	46	30

Further, if we use all the data available on the status of children, such as that presented in the document *School Age Demographics*[1], we see clearly that Bennett's "top 10 states" have low numbers not only of children in poverty but also of single-parent households, single teen parents, and students with limited proficiency in English. For example, Bennett's number-two state, North Dakota, has both the lowest number of single-parent households in the country and the lowest number of students with limited proficiency in English. It has the fourth-lowest number of single teen parents and the 20th-lowest number of children in poverty. Number-four Nebraska has the fourth-lowest number of single-parent households, the 16th-lowest number of children in poverty, the 12th-lowest number of single teen parents, and the ninth-lowest number of students with limited proficiency in English. If we look at a composite of the 10 states, their *average* rankings for each of the four categories are: seventh lowest in the country for single-parent households, 15th lowest for children in poverty, 12th lowest for single teen parents, and 17th lowest for students with limited proficiency in English.

What about Bennett's bottom line that more money does not translate into a better education? For example, Bennett's top 10 states average 1,040 on the SAT while averaging nearly $5,000 in per-pupil expenditures. But as a group they have only 9% of their seniors taking the SAT. The 10 highest-spending states have a lower average SAT score (903) and spend nearly $8,000 per student. But nearly 66% of their high school seniors take the SAT. So which argument do you want to make—that "increased educational spending doesn't translate into higher SAT scores" or that, "money aside, if a high percentage of students take the test, then the group is going to include a lot of non-college bound 'C' students who will bring down the composite scores"? If what we want as a society is high SAT scores, then all we have to do is deny low-income students access to the test. On the other hand, if we want large numbers of students to take the test and do well on it, then we're probably talking about major boosts in public spending to help low-income students overcome the disadvantages associated with their economic plight. Bennett can't have it both ways.

Had he looked, Bennett would have found the correlation between poor

SAT scores and school-age poverty rates. On our list of 23 states where the SAT is the more widely used college entrance examination, only one of the top-scoring states (California) has any significant percentage of its children coming to school from families living in poverty. Stated differently, of the 10 states with the greatest number of school-age children in poverty, only California ranks on our list of 23 top-scoring SAT states.

But even if we use Feistritzer's data—without the benefit of Bennett's spin—we can see that money does seem to make a positive difference in student achievement. For example, if you compare poor states to wealthy states, the latter outscore the former by an average of 60 points and have more students taking the test than low-spending states (about 10 times more).

Further, if we are looking for improvement over time, Feistritzer's data reveal that, of the 15 states that increased their share of the budget for education, six are on Bennett's top-10 high-achievement list. So, while expenditures are generally lower for these states, they are putting more effort into paying for education than most other states relative to their ability, and they seem to be getting something for it.

The five lowest-spending states in 1972 (Alabama, Arkansas, Mississippi, Kentucky, and Tennessee) have improved their relative ranking since then by an average of six ranking places. They also improved their SAT scores by 68 points: from an average of 936, with 5.6% taking the test in 1972, to an average of 1,004, with an average of 8.6% taking the test. Would it be inappropriate for us to put our own spin on the data and suggest that increased spending yields increased SAT scores?

Inappropriate or not, we have to believe that the public is getting tired of the manipulation of data to support arguments on both sides of tough policy issues. What we need is a database that clearly forces fact and fiction to part company.

Emerson Elliott, long-time commissioner of the National Center for Education Statistics, U.S. Department of Education, knows statistics. And he's having the time of his life as Congress spends more and more money every year to collect better and better education statistics, partially in response to the misuse of the data by critics of education. But even with additional dollars, Elliott readily acknowledges the limitations of more education data. He points out that there is no well-known analytic system for education data. And even if there were, could anyone be sure it would be technically sophisticated, ideologically unbiased, and nonpartisan? As Elliott has said, "The temptation to cheat doesn't pass with youth." Some people, he suggests (without mentioning William Bennett by name), will always interpret data to promote their cause or beliefs. [2]

Given the tendency of public school critics to use data in their attacks on the enterprise, the public has come to believe that we have a crisis in education. We know better. Most of our schools are not in a crisis mode. Most are doing an outstanding job. But clearly, we have a crisis developing in those schools attempting to educate large percentages of sick, hungry, and abused children. That's the message we ought to be delivering — heavens knows, we certainly have the data to support it.

While educators struggle to improve education for all children, Bennett and the other drive-by education critics continue to fire their rhetorical silver bullets, worrying little about the damage they may cause. It's time they holster their weapons. Making educators wince and duck may be good sport, but it isn't contributing to school improvement.

References

1. *School Age Demographics: Recent Trends Pose New Educational Challenges* (Washington, D.C.: General Accounting Office, August 1993).
2. Emerson J. Elliott, John H. Ralph, and Brenda J. Turnbull, "Monitoring the Nation's Educational Health," *Phi Delta Kappan*, March 1993, pp. 520-522.

෨෪

Co-authored by E. Joseph Schneider. Reprinted with permission from
Phi Delta Kappan, June 1994, pp. 779-792.

Governance. For many districts it has become a four-letter word, as superintendent and board fight for ascendance. The fact is, to work effectively, the two must create a symbiotic relationship. Here are a few ideas.

૨૦

A Lens on Leadership

Micromanagement, mistrust, misunderstanding—here's a close look at how boards and superintendents (sometimes) get along

Any time school boards and superintendents start talking about their mutual relationship, the discourse is apt to be titled "Sleeping With the Enemy." And there's no magic that will make the relationship work.

Of course, I've never been a school board member. But over the course of my 17 years in the superintendency, I served with from 40 to 50 different board members and spent the equivalent of two and a half work years in board meetings. From my perspective, there is nothing easy about being either a superintendent or a school board member. One of the difficulties you face in both jobs is that all the easy problems have been solved before they reach you. The situations that do make it all the way up the ladder to the top decision makers are apt to be thankless, and your efforts often go unappreciated.

But we have to recognize that we — board members and superintendents — are in it together. Unfortunately, we often end up going at each other rather than working together. If I might make a radical suggestion, we ought to be supporting one another more than we have historically.

WHERE PROBLEMS ARISE

With all the factors that already conspire to make things tough for school board members and superintendents — not the least of which is the charge of micromanagement on the part of school boards — the last thing we need is to add to the complexities and difficulties among ourselves. But here are several ways in which we do exactly that:

➤ **Lack of clarity regarding expectations.** Say I send you off with instructions to find me a dog. You bring back a dog, and I say, "Well, you brought back a small dog, and I really wanted a big dog." So you go off again and bring back a big dog, and I say, "Well I want a big black dog, and you brought me back a big white dog." So off you go again and come back with a big black dog, to which I say, "I wanted a big black dog with long hair, and you brought me . . . ." Of course, this story could go on forever — and so, unfortunately, could the misunderstandings that can arise when people don't make their expectations clear.

As superintendents and board members, we sometimes fail to be specific about just what we are looking for. The result can be a lot of wasted time and unnecessary frustration on the part of the people trying to carry out the task. Establishing clearly understood goals about what you want to do as an organization makes a lot of difference.

➤ **Mistrust between board and superintendent.** Lack of trust ensures problems in the relationship. Yet, regrettably, some school boards see the superintendent as the enemy, and vice versa. And that's counterproductive: If we are not working together, there is little we can accomplish.

≈ Rules written in shifting sands. Try to picture a baseball game in which the rules are subject to change the moment the ball leaves the pitcher's hand. For instance, a ball caught on one hop suddenly is considered an out. School systems sometimes play a version of that game. What we need from each other is a sense of constancy, a sense that we can depend on one another to play by the same rules tomorrow that we used today, an assurance that we won't be surprised.

≈ The narrow agenda. Unfortunately, we are seeing in school systems more of what I call the "I- me-mine" theory of leadership. You've heard it — it's *my* community, *my* school, *my* child. This phenomenon is the reverse of the NIMBY syndrome, or Not In My Back Yard — unless, of course, the matter in question is considered positive or desirable. Then I want it in *my* back yard.

But as you know, this approach does not work very well from either a board member's or a superintendent's perspective. You have to be there for all the children — not just those from one part of town. Real leadership requires a more balanced approach that acknowledges we are here for a broader constituency.

≈ Loose lips. Talking out of school — releasing confidential information from executive sessions, for example — is a sure way to create problems.

One of the rules I always tried to keep as a superintendent was that when one board member knew something, all board members knew it. It used to drive some of my board members crazy. They would ask me a question, and the next week they would see the answer to their question sent to all their colleagues. But I believed that was the only way I could really make sure everybody understood. I was trying to be as evenhanded as possible; I wanted to make sure people who needed the information got it, and that one board member didn't have a lot of inside, privileged information that might then be used politically.

≈ Sabotage. This problem takes many forms, including asking the answer-less — "Are you still beating your wife?" kind of question. Occasionally, someone in a meeting will ask you such questions ("When do you think you will be able to solve this nagging problem?") knowing that, no matter what you say, it's going to be wrong. And that's not a terribly helpful thing to do.

Similarly, board members can send their superintendents off on a hopeless mission — asking them to solve a knotty problem everyone knows has no real solution, such as a controversial racial situation. The superintendent can play another version of that game, which is to set up the board and create a situation in which, no matter what happens, the board looks bad. Sabotage directed either way undermines the efforts and goals of the organization.

Ambiguity of responsibility. Whose job is it to do what? There really is no way to carve the boundaries in stone, and that is a fundamental problem. Take micromanagement: There are times when the board has to get involved in management issues, and there are times when the superintendent wants the board out of that area. (Personnel issues are a classic example.) The more the two sides talk to one another about such problem areas — including overlaps in responsibility — and the more they do so in a manner that is open, honest, and mutually supportive, the more smoothly the organization will function.

Bickering board members. Battling board members pose a fundamental problem because, once the conflict goes public, it really doesn't matter who wins and who loses. When board members are at odds, the district always loses. So when you have differences with your colleagues, the organization will be better off if you keep the matter from the public.

Superintendent as superhero. Where is it written that when you hire a superintendent, that person must be a superhero? But look at almost any employment ad announcing a search for a superintendent. If you could find anybody who could do everything the board lists as a requirement, you wouldn't have a superintendent, you'd have a deity.

The fact is, school boards often look for a superintendent who can do everything and be all things to all people. And, of course, that's not humanly possible. So when the bloom is off the rose and you've found that the person you hired doesn't walk on water — and more likely struggles to tread water — you need to be understanding and supportive. This is a human enterprise, after all.

KEEPING IT CLICKING ON ALL CYLINDERS

No article on this subject would be complete — not to mention credible — without a list of do's and don'ts. So here, from the point of view of a recovering superintendent, are some ways school board members can help keep the school system running smoothly:

✦ **Look at the big picture.** Board members should be looking at the school system through a wide-angle lens, not a microscope. Don't focus on the very specific, minor parts of the organization. Focus on the overall picture. If you are not doing so, and the superintendent is not doing so, nobody is going to.

✦ **Identify problems and issues, not solutions.** Board members are elected to serve as the question people, not the answer people. You are there to identify the big issues; the solutions are up to the professional educators.

✦ **Determine what should be taught, not how it should be taught.** Many board members have a tendency to want to go in and tell teachers how they ought to conduct the reading program. Instead, you should concern yourselves with determining what kind of reading program you want to have. More broadly, what kind of curriculum do you want to have? That is where you, as board members, directly reflect the community's value system.

As a corollary, it's your responsibility to establish policy, but leave the carrying out of that policy — the day-to-day workings of the operation — to others.

✦ **Ask questions.** Education is a complex enterprise, giving rise to many questions that need to be answered by the staff. A good board is one that takes advantage of its resources to find the answers to those questions.

✦ **Don't make the superintendent a "go-fer."** There were times when I really thought we could have hired somebody at $4 or $5 an hour to do what I was being ask to do, as opposed to what I thought my job was — to lead the organization.

Once, I received a call from a board member who wanted to know what we were going to do about the gophers in the lawn at one of our high schools. I said, "We'll turn the problem over to the grounds people." About a week later, he asked if I'd dealt with that gopher problem yet. But the board's involvement should have stopped with reporting the problem.

What School Boards and Corporate Boards Have in Common

Board service in the corporate world holds some lessons for school boards — or so I've concluded from my reading of the works of management expert Peter Drucker.

Drucker points out that the members of a company's board of directors are the legally constituted representative of the owners. The same holds true in a school system: Essentially, a school board represents the owners of the schools, the public at large.

When I was a superintendent, I always tried to keep in mind that the board members were there to represent the values of the community that elected them. When board members did not follow my recommendations on specific matters, I realized in hindsight that in almost every case, they had made the right decision — the decision the community would consider appropriate. Superintendents have to remember that what they consider the "right" answer from a professional standpoint isn't necessarily the right answer for the school district, and the board, through the wisdom of its collective understanding, usually knows the difference.

Drucker has also written about the decline in the power of corporate boards of directors, and it occurs to me a parallel phenomenon is occurring in education. Drucker attributes the decline to three factors:

If the superintendent has a track record of ignoring board concerns, there's a bigger hole in the district than the one the gopher is digging.

❧ Help act as a buffer. Both boards and superintendents should act as buffers between the staff and the public. When I was a superintendent, I always

---

1. *A divorce of ownership from control.* As companies have expanded, the ownership of the company is no longer directly connected to the control of the company. The same is true of education. Court orders, state and federal laws, teacher unions — these and other factors have wrested control of education away from its true owners, making the school board's role more difficult than it used to be.

2. *The complexity of the operation of the organization.* Small or large, all school districts are complex. Public education involves increasing numbers of stakeholders and embraces a growing multitude of problems, and this complexity also complicates the school board's role.

3. *The difficulty of finding good people to serve on the board.* School board members volunteer their time to serve the children and the community, yet they increasingly are the targets of abuse, both at public meetings and in their private lives. It's no wonder people see serving on the school board as a thankless task.

But it shouldn't be. The school board — like the corporate board Drucker writes of — is the essence of leadership. Drucker says a board of directors is responsible for defining the company's business, approving objectives, and determining whether those objectives have been met. Similarly, a school board looks after the spirit of the organization — that intangible essence that says, "This is what our school district is about, and this is how we measure its success."—P.H.

---

believed part of my job was to help shield the organization from the day-to-day pressures of direct community contact so that school staff members could get the job done. School boards, I believe, should serve a similar function.

⅏ Solve problems a level above where they appear to be. I'm not talking staff levels here; I'm talking philosophy, so stay with me. Problems can be classified into three basic areas: mission, resources, and personnel. The trouble is, what might seem to be a resource problem often is a mission problem. Yet we attempt to solve it at the personnel level. So we have dropped down a level instead of moving up a level in terms of how we try to solve the problem.

Move your search for a solution up to the next highest level, then look behind the problem and say, "Why does this really seem to be a problem? Why are we having a resource problem? Maybe because we haven't thought out our priorities in terms of what our mission is. Why do we seem to have a personnel problem? Maybe we don't have the resources to have enough people to do that job."

Always try to look at the problem a level above where it seems to be.

⅏ Strive for clarity. Set clear expectations and look for clear results (see my shaggy dog story). A board's most difficult job is articulating what it wants the school district to accomplish — and how the board will know when those goals have been accomplished. That is a task we often avoid because it is so difficult.

The business we're in is complex in terms of figuring out how it works and how to interpret success or failure. But that's what real leadership at the board level is all about — helping the superintendent and the senior staff clarify the characteristics of success for the rest of the organization.

⅏ Choose a good leader. The most important role of a good board is always to choose a good superintendent, and to work with him, support him, and hold him — or her — accountable for results. I always looked forward to my evaluations with the board because I believed that was the one time in the year when board members and I were able to have a clear conversation about their collective expectations of me and how I was doing. The rest of the year, the superintendent faces as many different sets of individual expectations as there are board members, and that can be much more difficult to deal with effectively.

Certainly there are any number of other useful suggestions for ensuring a smoother working relationship between the board and superintendent, and, in turn, a better-functioning school system. The bottom line is that we must forswear our long-established practice of circling the wagons and then firing inward. Enough people are taking potshots at us already without us sniping at one another. Let's take aim instead at ways the community's elected school representatives and appointed top administrator can work together for the benefit of the entire system.

In this piece, which appeared in *Phi Delta Kappan,* I took a step back from the rush toward privatization to point out a few holes in the theory. I think that an increase in public school privatization is somewhat inevitable as niche companies prove their worth. The role of superintendents, then, will be to broker those activities, to ensure quality and equity, and to ask the tough questions.

❧

Making Watches or Making Music

Over the past several years there has been an explosion of interest in privatizing public education in this country. Denis Doyle's proposal is but the latest salvo in the continuing campaign to persuade the public that privatizing is the solution to all our problems. However, the premise that the quality of schools has somehow deteriorated over time and that only eternal intervention will save them is flawed. The fundamental issue is that the schools have been affected by a great many external problems that are beyond their capacity to solve without cooperation from the broader community.

Private sector management of schools is not, in and of itself, a bad idea. Unfortunately, it's far too early in the process to say whether it will help schools respond to the external challenges they face or whether it will be just one more simple solution to a complex problem that simply won't work. Certainly in the noninstructional areas, such as busing, lunchrooms, and custodial support, private sector management has been around in school systems for a long time. However, these three areas are most closely aligned with private sector practices and can most easily yield efficiencies. There is nothing inherently educational in running a bus, serving a meal, or sweeping a floor. These are all activities that have been done broadly throughout our society, and certainly educators have no special claim to being able to do them better. The crux of the debate comes when one considers the possibility of private sector profiteers assuming control of the tasks associated with teaching children.

Doyle wonders whether educators will "reject the opportunity to use the services of private management companies." He thus assumes that private management is presenting an opportunity. And that assumption must be tested before anyone spends a lot of time or money on privatizing schools. Clearly, Doyle is a true believer in privatizing and is thoroughly sold on its glories. However, it would behoove all educators to look at this issue most carefully before jumping off the end of the dock.

Doyle does ask some useful questions, such as, "Will reliable and competent 'education management' companies enter and remain in the market?" I believe that this is the $64,000 question. But we should also ask the companion question, "What do we mean by 'reliable' and 'competent' in this context?" School boards and superintendents had better have a good feel for what these words mean before they sign over the education of children to a private firm.

Doyle states that, while we feel we have a diverse education system, there is really a striking absence of diversity in the system, from state to state and from district to district. That's debatable and depends on how one understands "diversity." Having served as a superintendent in various states and districts across the country, I can testify that, while classrooms tend to look similar from state to state, what goes on inside them varies dramatically by quality of teaching, by resources available, and by community expectations and other social factors. Furthermore, many of the privatizers would like to use the private school model as a beacon for modifying public school when, in fact, private schools are struggling with questions of innovation and creativity at least as profound as those being confronted by public schools. Indeed, the only schools less diverse than public schools are private ones.

Doyle raises the question of whether private sector instructional management will improve schools. This too is a central question and one that must be answered before any wholesale movement to private management takes place. Having worked in schools affected by poverty, racism, and all forms of social problems, I find it hard to see how private companies will do any better than public agencies at addressing such issues while improving instruction.

Doyle points out that it's cheaper and easier for private sector providers to own, service, and operate a bus or the food service than it is for a school system. That is true for one simple reason. Private sector employers tend to pay their employees less and offer fewer benefits than public sector employers. While this is clearly part of a major economic movement in this country, it does have one unintended consequence: It creates what have come to be called "McJobs." In essence, it lowers the standard of living for those who hold these jobs. So, while the employers save money, society may not be benefitting quite as richly because people have less to spend and a lower standard of living. Moreover, many of these people will be parents, and so the standard of living of the children served by the schools will be driven down as well.

Doyle does concede that there are some public functions that should remain public, such as the maintenance of a police force or an army. But he does not concede the same for education.

Moreover, he questions whether government needs to own and operate the means of production in order to see that services are provided wisely and well. One of the fundamental questions we must deal with here is, "What is being produced by education?" Critics have long seemed to imply that the goal of education is to produce higher test scores. That is how we get international and state-by-state comparisons of test scores, viewed by some as the sole measures of whether one state or country is more effective than another. The fact is that education's role in production is to produce a *better society*. Whether that will happen through privatizing is clearly a debatable question.

Doyle raises the specter of special pleading by interest groups as one reason that the schools are not privatized. He rightly points out that the real issue is what will better serve the students. While there can be no doubt that a great many special interests cluster around schools—including the interests of administrators, of teachers concerned with their jobs and job satisfaction, and of parents and their array of chosen issues—it is also clear that the goal of creating a profit for a private company could certainly be construed as a special interest. Whether making a profit is any more noble or less dangerous than serving other special interests that currently exist in schools is another question that Doyle fails to raise or answer. And will a profit motive translate into what is best for children?

Doyle states that "by any set of measures our schools — particularly our major urban school systems — are in trouble. Unfortunately, he does not talk about why they are in trouble. That seems to be the real problem with the analyses of many of those who propose radical school reform. The reality is that schools are troubled today because our society is in trouble. Over the last 30 years we have gone from a society that provided children with a setting straight out of "Leave It to Beaver" to a society that holds up Beavis and Butthead and Bart Simpson as juvenile icons.

The shift in the condition of children, both in terms of their value to society and with regard to the support systems surrounding them, is a fundamental reason why so many of our large-city school systems are encountering difficulty. It's very difficult to hold off a "rising tide of mediocrity" by shoveling water back into the sea, but that's akin to what many of our schoolpeople are being asked to do in places were resources are inadequate to meet the social deterioration surrounding them. It is not at all clear that privatizing will solve these problems or do any better a job of dealing with the other intractable issues facing schools than public management has done.

While it is clear that the private sector has brought many fine things to this country, it is not at all clear that everything the private sector has done to and for children has been useful. In many ways the private sector has contributed its share to the corruption of children's values, through advertising and the media blitz to which children are daily subjected. In essence, we now see a country in which our children know the price of everything and the value of nothing. Furthermore, through the private sector we have created a situation in which we spend more money on cat food than we do on textbooks. We've also created a throwaway society, and, unfortunately, the children in our poorer neighborhoods have become part of the refuse. Under a privatized system, a fundamental question is, Who will protect our children?

One suggestion Doyle offers rankles me personally. I refer to his implication that it's time for schoolpeople to "engage serious, accomplished, and thoughtful management consultants to improve both instructional and noninstructional management" of schools. By itself, this is a wonderful idea. However, Doyle goes on to state that it's "a commentary on public schools themselves that such a course of action must be urged upon them."

With all due respect to Doyle, I did just what he advises more than a decade ago — without his urging — while I was superintendent in Princeton, New Jersey. I did the same thing in Tucson, Arizona, a few years later.

Doyle is absolutely correct in pointing to the value of an outside view of things for improving management. However, he may not be aware of the likelihood that outsiders will find the schools' problems just as schoolpeople themselves do. At least when I brought in management consultants, their response was that the schools were doing a tremendous job with their limited resources and that they had few real suggestions to offer for significant savings. In fact, these outside managers, once they learned the way schools must operate, found it remarkable that schools do as well as they do under the circumstances. To the extent that some school leaders are reluctant to engage this outside viewpoint, then Doyle has a point.

However, merely bringing in outside consultants may not improve efficiency nearly as much as it may increase the credibility of the jobs schools are already doing.

Doyle also points out that schools should consider using quality management techniques. Again, as head of the American Association of School Administrators, I found this suggestion a little difficult to deal with because we have had an extensive program that has gone on for several years to help schools institute total quality management. In fact, we had a good and strong working relationship with the late W. Edwards Deming. I think Doyle would be amazed at what schoolpeople in many communities are already doing.

Doyle also hit schools for not making more use of technology because schoolpeople argue that they can't afford it. He points out that technology creates the very efficiencies that would allow schools to afford more of it. However, in the private sector, when the company is making a transition from one form of manufacturing to another, specific funds are always budgeted for transitional costs. In education, one rarely sees any significant money put into making a transition from one way of doing business to another. The burden of such changes as shifting to greater use of technology is put on the backs of teachers and administrators, while they continue with their regular jobs as well. Business would never operate in this way. If businesspeople are serious about moving into education, they need to understand that these costs must be built into any activities they attempt.

There are two other issues that one must consider when looking at Doyle's proposal. First, it has been my experience that, while there is a call to privatize public functions in this country, when one starts to talk about whether schools should become more entrepreneurial in dealing with child-related businesses — such as providing after-school day care or preschool programs — a great hue and cry goes up from private sector providers of those services. They feel that schools have unfair advantage. In essence, while it may be perfectly fine to privatize public functions, it seems abhorrent to the private sector to suggest that one might want to "public-ize" private functions. If we're going to go full bore into this debate, we have to accept that what's sauce for the goose is sauce for the gander.

There is also an interesting issue raised by William Baumol, a Princeton University economist. Baumol is an expert on why public services cost more than private services. Baumol points out that there is a thing called "cost disease," which is not caused by inefficiency or ineptitude. Instead, "cost disease" arises because improvements in productivity are very difficult to bring about in government services, but much easier to achieve in private endeavors. This is simply because the work government workers do is labor-intensive and does not lend itself to the improvements created by technology in the same way as do capital-intensive industries in the private sector.

For example, Baumol points out that 76 workers in 1990 could make as many cars as 100 workers in 1979, and 42 workers could produce as many computers as 100 workers produced. Moreover, the 1990 products were also of higher quality. However, for teachers to experience this kind of productivity increase, we would have to increase class size from 25 in 1979 to 33 in 1990. And while some of this has gone on, it has not happened without a decline in the quality of service. The soaring class sizes in some states have not led to improved performance, in large part because the teachers are coping not only with more children but with more difficult children at the same time.

In fact, Baumol points out, the deterioration in government performance does not result from bureaucratic inefficiency. It comes about simply because improvements in productivity are spread unevenly throughout our economy. We must spend a greater share of our income to maintain the constant level of services in some sectors and a smaller share to maintain a constant level in others. Baumol uses as his example the fact that it takes a person the same amount of time to play a Scarlatti harpsichord solo today as it did 260 years ago. Yet 260 years ago, a craftsman would make a single watch in the time it took to play 100 solos. Today, a single watch can be manufactured in less time than it takes for a single performance of the Scarlatti solo. This means that in 260 years the price of a concert ticket has risen about 100 times as fast as the price of a watch. Thus watches are no longer a luxury, while concert tickets are. However, no one blames this difference on "bureaucratic bloat" in the music industry.

In considering Baumol's analysis, one must quickly come to the conclusion that, when privatizing is presented as a solution to education's so-called inefficiencies, we are witnessing the proposed invasion of the watchmakers who want to play Scarlatti solos. But simply playing songs faster or improving their "efficiency" by leaving out some of the notes won't work — in music or education. If the children are to benefit, the harpsichord-playing watchmakers will need to play the music of education "prettier" as well. And the music review jury is still out on that.

ॐ

Reprinted with permission from *Phi Delta Kappan*, October 1994, pp. 133-135.

A national gathering of educational leaders and thinkers who got together to worry about the condition of schools and the issue of equity allowed me to think and write about something that is too often ignored in these discussions — context.

ॐ

School Reform Through a Wide-Angle Lens: The Consideration of Context

Education reform in this country is off-base because we keep trying to fix the wrong problem. We assume that the problem lies within the school and that by "fixing" the school we can fix the problem. A great deal of time and effort has been spent trying to improve upon what we have historically done in school and finding better ways to measure this. This is based on the assumption that schools are failing children. But bad assumptions make bad policy. It is our society that is failing our children and we must look at this issue more broadly; we cannot fix the schools outside of their societal context. As Ernest Boyer reminds us in a recent Carnegie report, we cannot have islands of academic excellence in a sea of community indifference.

Until America is willing to consider the context within which schools exist as a part of the problem, our efforts at reform will fall short. Creating "standards," "benchmarks," or "outcomes" is useful. We need to know where we are going. Moving towards more authentic assessment makes sense. But before trying to go somewhere else, we need to better understand where we are now. I was once told by someone who worked on a ranch that cattle could never be fattened by being weighed, they had to be fed. Likewise, assessing children's performances does not make them achieve more. Yet, much of our reform effort in this country has revolved around the idea that we can "weigh" children into better performance. Instead, we must convince children, and those who serve them, that we understand their problems and are willing to support them in dealing with those problems. This does not mean that we expect less of those who have difficulty; it does mean that we must recognize that some need more support than others to reach the goal.

Those who make policy in this country and those who must carry it out in the classroom live in two different solar systems that are moving apart at the speed of light. We must find ways to connect the "top down" strategies with the "bottom up" strategies and create mechanisms for improving children's lives outside of school.

The condition of many of the children in this country is horrendous. This is particularly true of children living in inner cities and rural communities. The poverty rate for children is increasing dramatically: More than one in five children is now living in poverty. America's child poverty rate is three times the average of other industrialized countries. A generation ago, the poorest in our society were the elderly. Today, children are six times more likely to be poor than the elderly. The United Nations Children's Fund (UNICEF) report, *The Progress of Nations*, attributes this to the "failure of tax and transfer policies to mitigate poverty to the same degree [in the United States] as in other industrialized countries."[1]

Poverty is an economic problem, but it has tragic human overtones. Each year 10,000 children in the United States die as a direct result of living in poverty. Sen. Christopher Dodd, D-Conn., has suggested that whether we look at the poverty rate, immunization statistics, or school readiness, it is plain that many children are growing up in an environment that completely thwarts success in life. Violence towards children has escalated dramatically: Three children a day die of child abuse. Over the last 13 years we have lost 80,000 children to gun deaths, thousands more than we lost during the 25 years of the Vietnam conflict.

And what has been our policy? We have had none. We have failed to develop a national children's policy and this has led to some very strange outcomes. Our pets have a better chance of being inoculated than do our children; we spend more money on cat food than we spend on textbooks. Under President Bush, we developed a national goal that called for all children to come to school ready to learn. But he and his successor have done nothing to raise the estimated $30 billion it would cost to implement that goal.

Meanwhile, the schools must cope with the reality that our children have gone from a world of "Leave It to Beaver" to one of "Leave It to Beavis." In 1960, when "Leave It to Beaver" was popular, about 60 percent of American families resembled the Cleavers; they had a working father and a mother who stayed home to tend the children. Today nearly one-half of our children are "latch-key kids."

In addition, schools are very disconnected from the changing nature of the workplace, just as employers are very disconnected from the changing environment of children. Employers cannot understand why schools are not turning out a better product, and schools have not kept up with the changing demands of the workplace. The skills that many jobs require call for a much more sophisticated worker than was necessary on the factory floor. Even doing the same job today is more complex than it was a generation ago. In 1960, 20 percent of the jobs in this country required a high school education. Today, 80 percent require it.

Merely raising standards will lead to failure and frustration. Connections must be made between the two realities. What is needed is a much more realistic assessment of the needs of children and a commitment to meeting those needs.

To achieve this, I believe we need an investment strategy. An "investment trust fund" could be created that would go towards providing a minimal base of support for prenatal and postnatal health care, nutrition, and family support. This "investment trust" could come from a national payroll tax; a fraction of 1 percent could raise between $25 and $30 billion a year. This money could then be turned back to communities, on a formula basis for distribution, to support the most needy children. This would allow schools to concentrate resources on changing how they deliver education.

Suggesting a payroll tax at this particular time may seem naive. After all, the nation is focused on deficit reduction. However, it is time that we invested in the future of our children. Developing such a concept will take time, and gaining adequate support for passage will take even more time, but we should not wait to begin the process.

Once we have taken care of the basic needs of children, we must concentrate on changing our schools. Schools are doing a better job than ever of carrying out their historic mission. The problem is that it is the wrong mission. We are still treating children as if they come from the Cleaver household and are going to work on the assembly line. We must train a different kind of child for a very different world. This calls for a radical transformation of the schools into personalized places that provide for different learning styles, and that connect to the real world of work.

We must empower those working in schools to carry out the task at hand. Strategies of deregulating and moving decisions closer to the child are appropriate, but we must continue to provide "scaffolds" of support. Merely trying to reform one school at a time throws schools to the vagaries of conditions outside of their control and breaks down any opportunities for synergy. Most importantly, we as a nation must join in a crusade for our children. It must involve a commitment on the part of schools to change to meet the reality of a different world, and it must involve a commitment on the part of society to shoulder some of the responsibility for supporting children. We must move away from talking about "those" children and "my" children and begin talking about "our" children.

Anything short of this kind of commitment dooms schools to failure in contending with the context the children bring to us.

Endnote
[1] United Nations Children's Fund, *The Progress of Nations* (New York: UNICEF, 1993).

❧

Reprinted by permission of *Dædulus, Journal of the American Academy of Arts and Sciences*, from the issue entitled, "American Education: Still Separate, Still Unequal," Fall 1995, Vol. 124, No. 4, pp. 169-172.

The governors and business leaders got together and decided to fix schools. But they left some things out: schoolpeople and an understanding of the issues. I hate stupidity in almost any form, but I particularly despise it when it comes cloaked in platitudes and condescension.

ว∿

The Blab Meets the Blob: Summitry, School Reform, and the Role of Administrators

I recently had the opportunity to visit an old school in Dayton, Ohio. It was a preserved model of the schools that dotted the country in the last century. While there, our group of administrators and partners was subjected to lessons given by a teacher who taught us the old-fashioned way. While the whole experience was fascinating, especially the evidence about those things that have and have not changed, the most interesting moment came when we were all asked to read, out loud, simultaneously from different passages in the venerable McGuffey Reader. Imagine the noise! This cacophony of sound was known as "blab school," and it is amazing that anyone learned to read in those "good old days." And for those who may be wishing for simpler times, and who think that readers were better then, we must note that reading literacy in America is higher today than at any point in history. The least literate portion of our population is the elderly, who were subjected to these methods in their childhood.

The real lesson I received revolved around the fact that we were visiting the school during the same week the nation's governors and business leaders were meeting at the national education summit in Palisades, N.Y., to determine the future of American education. The rhetoric as a result of the summit was very reminiscent of the meaningless babble I heard at "blab school." I had to wonder how a group of reportedly intelligent and well-informed people could get together and restate so much bad information, and create an atmosphere so counterproductive to the future of education. (See *Education Week*, April 3, 1996.)

Let me make one thing quite clear. I believe that higher standards and wider and more effective use of technology are absolutely essential to improving education in this country. I also completely agree that a major transformation of schools must occur if our children are to have any chance at all of a successful future. I salute the business community and governors for focusing on these things and for drawing attention to them.

What I cannot salute is the random havoc that they perpetrated on the millions of educators who are being asked to make the adjustments necessary. This violence displayed itself as unwarranted criticism and ignorance about the context within which these educators currently labor. It is hard to understand how anyone can believe that people can be bludgeoned to greatness. I am reminded of a sign I once saw that pictured slaves in the galley of a ship, madly rowing to the beat of a whip, with the slogan, "The beatings will continue until morale improves." If educational improvement could come from mindless and mistaken criticism, the schools in this country would have improved a long time ago.

It is important to note that the handful of so-called education advisers invited to the conference were relegated to the back rows and not given microphones to allow their participation. Educators were all but left out of the process. It was assumed that those doing the work today, and who will be asked to carry out the ideas developed, had little to contribute to the discussion. The sheer arrogance and stupidity of this thinking can best be exemplified by a modest suggestion that we have a national summit on the failure of state government to address the needs of children, the inequity of state education funding, and the failure of the American business community to provide adequate high-paying jobs for young people. Further, that we conduct this summit by gathering educators together, invite a few token governors and business leaders, and sit them in the back of the room so they can witness the criticism. It might make us feel better, but it wouldn't help improve the ideas under discussion.

The fact is that society is a complex social system. Good education starts before children are born. They must have sound prenatal care and healthy mothers. Children must have a healthy and stimulating preschool experience provided by primary caregivers. They must go to schools that are adequately funded, with good teachers and safe environments. Their chances should not be determined by where their parents can afford to live. They must have parents who have incomes and who have not been "downsized" out of work. They must know that what they did in school will mean something to an employer. And they must have the possibility of a job that will give them an adequate living when they leave school. If all that can be made possible, then school reform will be a snap.

President Clinton was the only speaker at the conference who even acknowledged that when we speak of international comparisons, we must consider the different contexts facing children. Much of what he had to say made sense and was useful. Unfortunately, he fell in to the temptation to trash school leaders as being part of the problem.

School leaders have been under attack for a number of years. That was taken to new heights by former U.S. Secretary of Education William J. Bennett, who popularized the notion of the "blob" to designate all those hordes of administrators who were sucking the lifeblood out of schools and shifting money from classrooms to the "bureaucracy." He pointed out that half of the money in schools in America goes to the classroom and the other half to the bureaucracy. Even President Clinton uses the statistics from New York City that indicate only half of the money spent on education goes to classrooms. Without arguing over the statistics, it should be pointed out that few of the participants at the summit could survive a day of teaching in many of the schools in our cities.

What the president and others have failed to discuss is what that bureaucracy entails. When you examine the facts and shift those resources back to the classroom, you could make some difference. You could have smaller classes and higher-paid teachers. But you couldn't really shift it to the classroom, because you wouldn't have a classroom. Some of the "bureaucracy" money is money to pay for the building, to pay for heating the building, turning on the lights, getting the children to and from school, feeding them, keeping the building clean, putting textbooks on students' desks and computers in the back of the room. It pays for secretaries, counselors, special-education teachers, and psychologists. And yes, it pays for administrators.

How much? According to a study done by the Education Research Service, central-office administrators, the "bureaucracy," make up about 1.6 percent of the education workforce nationally. Another 2.9 percent of the workforce are building-level administrators. About 4.3 percent of district budgets go to administration, which ironically is almost exactly the same amount that went to administration in 1960—long before various federal and state mandates on equity and special education reshaped the education landscape and created myriad new requirements for oversight and monitoring. So, despite major new tasks, the "bureaucracy" hasn't gotten any bigger in the last 30 years.

It is more than ironic that a group of governors and chief executive officers would get together and, as part of their reform agenda, defame school leaders, since they, themselves, are all administrators. Perhaps I'm overreacting. Perhaps they really do understand the need for leadership. Perhaps they do believe that higher standards, improved performance, and better use of technology will require leadership and capacity-building. Perhaps they realize that someone has to connect top-down reform coming from the state level and bottom-up reform emanating from the building level. Perhaps they think that education is just too top-heavy and needs to be lean and mean, like government and business. Perhaps they need to visit the facts.

Currently, education has one manager for every 14.5 employees. Business ranges in manager-to-employee ratios from the transportation industry, which has 9.3 workers for every manager, to communications (the dreaded media), which has 4.7 workers for every manager. Public administration (which presumably includes the bailiwick of governors) employs one manager for every 3.6 employees. And, of course, this analysis does not factor in the reality that school administrators must also manage hundreds of students and their intensely interested parents, a challenge the private sector is mercifully spared.

The moral of this story is that people who live in glass houses ... well, you know the rest. People should not make presumptions about others based on their own situation, or at least they should have some facts before pontificating.

The real fact is that schools need to change dramatically to meet the new demands placed on them, so that every child can have a chance to grab the brass ring in a more complex and difficult social and economic setting. The fact is higher standards and better use of technology will help get us there. The fact is that all of us, politician, business leader, and educator, will have to work more closely together to make it happen. The fact is those who are doing the work now, and who must do the work of educating in the future, must be respected and empowered to accomplish it. And the fact is, change in any setting requires good leadership and sound management.

The good news from the summit is that, perhaps for the first time since we started on this long and tough journey toward school reform, a real consensus is starting to emerge around what a new mission for education might be. The other good news is that there is now a stated goal of the politicians and business leaders to roll up their sleeves and help with the heavy lifting.

The bad news is that, right now, we only have their rhetoric, much of it negative and based upon bad assumptions. No one is ready yet to say what it is we are going to do with the bottom third of our population who come to school hungry and ill-cared-for.

Governors can propose laws to change things. Business leaders can refuse to accept raw materials that don't fit their specifications. The fact is, parents send schools the best children they have and schools must educate them all. To do so, we must improve the process of educating. Higher standards and technology will help. We must also improve how we treat our children, so that they'll have a chance at education. At some point, perhaps we'll have a summit on how we can help our society improve the condition of its children. That will give all of us something to cheer about—then the "blabbing" will have some meaning.

§▲

Reprinted from *Education Week*, April 24, 1996.

I have increasingly come to believe that our salvation as school leaders will come from our ability to reach out and engage our communities. This piece points the way.

ॐ

Administrator Accessibility: Invite the Wolf for Coffee

A recent children's book turns around the story of the three little pigs. It seems, according to the author, that the wolf was simply misunderstood. The huffing and puffing that the pigs heard at their doors was a wolf with a bad head cold who only wanted to come in, sit by the fire and get warm.

This is a useful idea to keep in mind this year as school administrators and personnel look at the issue of engaging parents and involving their communities in the school setting. For far too long, schools and their constituents have been locked in a cold war of wills, each trying to keep the other from directly affecting the work and needs that each has. What needs to happen is a powerful collaboration between the two for the sake of the children we all care so much about.

SCHOOLS ARE PART OF THE VILLAGE

Lately, we have seen a battle of words about whether it takes a village or a family to raise a child. Anyone working with children knows the discussion is silly, because it takes all of us: a family, a village and a school—to raise a child. In any society, modern or primitive, the task of raising children is so complicated and demanding that it requires everyone's help but, with the deteriorating condition in many of our families and communities, the "village" has ceased to exist. One must then ask, "If it takes a village to raise a child, what does it take to raise a village?"

The foundation of a village begins with strong homes and strong families. Yet conditions facing our children and families today are, in many cases, beyond imagination. Hunger, sickness and abuse threaten children before they even have a chance to flourish. The breakdown of the extended family and the economic imperative of having two working parents or single parents working multiple jobs puts further stress on that foundation.

Indeed, it takes the whole village to raise the family, with contributions from all players, including the school. Better child-rearing and better education are vital to the continuity of a stable society to ensure that qualified workers, consumers and citizens are available so that all of us have a world in which to live and work.

Unfortunately, schools now bear a major burden in raising children. Currently, they are expected to teach the basics, provide for modern workplace skills, and inculcate strong values—all for about $33 per day, per child.

OPEN DOORS WITH COMMUNICATION

Given the complexity of creating the village and raising the child in today's environment, schools cannot afford to view the parents and the community as the big bad wolf banging at the door, wanting to come in and devour us. We must look at the prospect of inviting everyone into the house to be a part of the solution.

It is begun by doing more of what is already happening in the best situations. We need to have schools and their leaders do more risk-taking by initiating collaborations with unfamiliar community groups, and by opening up school decision making and governing to allow more input from parents, families, concerned adults and the community at-large.

We also have to open the school doors wider and to recognize that learning takes place beyond the classroom. We need to be visibly supportive by instituting policies and practices and fostering attitudes among educators that show that support.

Further, people in school need to be accessible and to provide better forms of communication between the school and the community at-large. Such things as linking teachers with parents by using more accessible and user-friendly approaches is a start.

Local cable and the new emerging forms of communications technology are also good ways of expanding and enhancing community communication. Schools are beginning to investigate electronic newsletters. Given the ever-increasing diversity of student populations, we have to recognize that multiple languages will now be a part of the process.

Schools must do more than just maintain better communication with the community. They must take the lead in integrating health and social services that must be made available to the children, youth and their families—preventive and problem-solving services.

A new coalition of "unfamiliar groups" has recently emerged in Washington that joins together school boards and superintendents, mayors, city councils and county commissioners. The Local Collaboration for Children and Youth works across local government and school lines to find ways of supporting the entire village and family through integrated and unified services.

SETTING A TONE
A school district leader must start with developing policies that set a tone for building this new infrastructure, in the school and in the community, to support actions designed to improve the lives of children through greater involvement of all sectors.

In short, school leaders in 1997 must look at the clamor and pressure coming from parents and the community for involvement in schools not as a problem, but as a rich possibility for improving what we do with children. School leaders must become weavers of a web of support around the children they serve. They must make the connections between individuals. It is clear that, when you stand in the middle of the road, you often get hit by the traffic going in both directions—but it's also a great place from which to direct traffic. Today's school leaders must be able to stand on their feet and make sure that the traffic continues to flow and does not damage the children we all serve.

What does it take to raise a village? It takes all of us — parents, educators, business people, relatives and neighbors — working together in concerted selflessness to create the support system for our children's dreams. In 1997, fling open the doors, and invite the wolf in for coffee.

è&

Reprinted from *School Planning and Management*.
(January 1997). pp. 24-25.